secret destinations

*In memory of my dear friend
Sue Kavals (30.9.57-27.01.04),
life, food and spa enthusiast*

Copyright © 2006 by Susie Donald.
Photographs copyright © 2006 Foodstyle Editions.
The moral right of the author has been asserted.

All rights reserved.
No portion of this book may be reproduced, stored in a retrieval system,
or transmitted in any form or by any means electronic, mechanical,
photocopying or otherwise without written permission of the publisher.

First published in 2006 by Foodstyle Editions
A division of Foodstyle
2-4 Mason Street,
Collingwood, Victoria, 3066,
Australia.
www.foodstyle.com.au

National Library of Australia
Cataloguing-in-Publication Data:

Donald, Susie
Secret Destinations: Asian Spa Cuisine.

ISBN 0-9750697-0-5

1. Cookery, Asian   2. Health Resorts- Asia
1. Ho, Edmond.   11. Poppy Fields.   111. Title

641.595

Photographs by Edmond Ho
Edited by Poppy Fields
Creative Direction by Susie Donald
Book design by Pfisterer + Freeman

Papers used by Foodstyle Editions are natural, recyclable products made
from wood grown in sustainable forests. The manufacturing processes
conform to the environmental regulations of the country of origin.

Colour Separation and Printing by SC (Sang Choy) International Pte Ltd
Distributed in Australia by Hardie Grant Books

secret destinations
ASIAN SPA CUISINE

susie donald   edmond ho

Thanks must go to our gracious hosts, the hotels and hotel management companies and their spa directors who have generously given their time and knowledge and availed us of unlimited staff to assist in the creation of Secret Destinations. This book would not have been possible without their spontaneous enthusiasm and support, not to mention their patience in awaiting its completion.

My special thanks go to the great chefs of these resorts who individually, yet together through their passion and imagination, have gathered the traditions, techniques and tastes of cooks from the various regions to help me create a collection of over 150 uncomplicated and delicious recipes.

The result is, I believe, a very unique book for cooks of all levels celebrating a healthful approach to one of life's primal pleasures.

Susie

Alfred Spieler, Sentosa Resort and Spa, Singapore

Christian Fogliani, Ana Mandara Resort, Nha Trang, Vietnam

Daniel Lentz, Amanpuri, Phuket, Thailand

Derek Watanabe, Four Seasons Resort at Chiang Mai, Thailand

Frank Ruidavet, Four Seasons Resort Maldives at Kuda Huraa, The Maldives

Hans-Ulrich Wismer, The Datai, Langkawi, Malaysia

Jomjai Klomkling, The Marriott, Bangkok, Thailand

Made Sukarmajaya, The Ibah, Ubud, Bali, Indonesia

Marc Miron, Four Seasons Resort Bali at Jimbaran Bay, Indonesia

Mark Patten, InterContinental Hong Kong

Matt Coates, Alila Ubud, Bali, Indonesia

Michael Poutawa, Evason, Phuket Resort, Phuket, Thailand

Patrick Duff, Hotel InterContinental Hong Kong

Raffles The Plaza, Singapore

Roland Hofman, Evason, Hua Hin Resort, Pranburi, Thailand

Sean O'Connor, The Legian, Bali, Indonesia

Simon Blaby, Alila Manggis, Bali, Indonesia

Vichit Mukara, The Oriental, Bangkok, Thailand

Vindex Valentino Tengker, Four Seasons Resort Bali at Sayan, Indonesia

Paisarn Cheewinsiriwat, Chiva Som, Hua Hin, Thailand

contents

8	preface
10	salus per aquum
12	what is spa cuisine?
14	cook's notes
16	the journey
18	Four Seasons Resort at Kuda Haraa, The Maldives
36	Hotel InterContinental Hong Kong
48	Ana Mandara Resort, Nha Trang, Vietnam
62	Chiva Som, Hua Hin, Thailand
70	The Oriental, Bangkok, Thailand
72	Evason Hua Hin Resort, Thailand
86	Four Seasons Resort at Chiang Mai, Thailand
96	Amanpuri, Phuket, Thailand
110	Evason Phuket Resort, Thailand
122	Marriott Resort and Spa, Bangkok, Thailand
136	The Datai, Langkawi, Malaysia
148	The Legian, Bali, Indonesia
162	Four Seasons Resort Bali at Jimbaran Bay, Indonesia
180	Four Seasons Resort Bali at Sayan, Indonesia
194	The Ibah, Ubud, Bali, Indonesia
206	Alila Manggis, Bali, Indonesia
222	Alila Ubud, Bali, Indonesia
232	Sentosa Resort and Spa, Singapore
242	Raffles the Plaza, Singapore
246	glossary
248	spa at home
253	recipe index
254	spa directory

preface

Based on the recognition that *fresh food* brings a restorative element of nature into our lives, Secret Destinations provides a connection between *nature* and *health*, by linking *diet and environment* and setting that connection in some of Asia's *finest tropical spa resorts*. Drawing on recipes from the most respected kitchens in the region, we take a *culinary journey* through the possibilities of *food, health, spiritualism* and destination.

The recent surge in the spa business is a sure sign that the modern world is once again seeking *refuge* in ancient therapies. By providing a *haven* from the frenetic pace of regular life, spas give us a place and time to re-connect with our *dreams, relax, and stimulate* our neglected *senses*.

And the resounding message they give us is clear – invest time in developing yourself and *take responsibility* for your own well-being. *Small changes* to your *diet and lifestyle* can make big differences in the long run, so take some advice from the experts and adopt a *healthy* approach to *the way you eat*.

Reading through the pages to come, you'll feel an irresistible urge to make a *pilgrimage*, find your *secret* destination, and *rub, scrub* and *eat* your way to *bliss*.

salus per aquum

Life is a journey with no map to guide us.

We all want or need to improve certain aspects of our diet or lifestyle to promote health and prevent disease. Urban living can almost be an illness in itself, characterised by the constant plague of fatigue, pain and restlessness.

More often than not our modern lifestyles leave us feeling the need to find sanctuary; to escape life's daily pressures and emerge revitalised. This sanctuary could be a place offering food for the soul and pampering for the body; somewhere to just kick back in style and soak up some culture in between naps. Or it may simply be a place with clean air or a spiritual backdrop, allowing space and time to think.

Some of us may be seeking personal growth in a number of realms, such as a more centred lifestyle, focus of mind or disciplined body.

But restoring that inner shine and outer glow requires us to draw time out from our busy lives. So put yourself first, invest in some feel-good therapies and natural healing, and embrace the lifestyle logic for the new millennium – SPA!

Originally the name "Spa" was given to a town in the Ardennes mountains, where its flowing waters drew people from far and wide to drink and bathe in it's curative powers. Today, the word spa refers to a combination of therapies for the body, mind and spirit that includes every holistic treatment from Ayurvedic cuisine to Zen meditation.

More than just an irresistible selection of unique destinations, the following pages may just be the key you're looking for, unlocking that path which leads to your own secret destination – a place not found on any map.

Now stop imagining...

what is spa cuisine?

The connection between what you eat and how you feel is not always obvious — until you improve your diet.

Small changes can make big differences in the long run.

Spa Cuisine is, by my definition, simple and nourishing; never fussy, but with great emphasis placed on freshness, lightness and balance. With a respect for the traditions, techniques and tastes of cooks from the various regions of this book, Spa Cuisine is light and appealing to those with modern day palates and an expectation of a healthy regime.

The food that we eat should be considered, up there with exercise, as one of the main features of our busy lifestyles: not something that should ever be neglected. In the pages to come you will see that healthful eating is not about boring bland food, but about controlling the balance and maintaining it.

By looking at how the body uses and stores food we can apply this knowledge to our menu planning. In the morning when our body is hungry and needs fuel, we have breakfasts that are satisfying and capable of releasing energy in preparation for the day ahead. By mid-morning the body needs a top-up of fluid so we would have a refreshing snack, such as a piece of fruit or a juice. The Spa Cuisine lunch, being the most substantial meal of the day should consist of a salad served with a high-in-protein, low-fat main course, then followed by a fruit-based dessert. Snacks in the afternoon should be thirst quenching and energizing, before an early evening dinner that comprises food that is light and easily digested.

I find that most Asian dishes can be modified and cooked in a way that is more healthful than the local version. Without losing too much in the translation, I have tailored the following recipes to work in with today's time constraints and create meals that are delicious, healthful and easy to prepare.

In true Asian style, all the recipes can be made in a tiny kitchen with a few basic utensils, by people with families to feed, after a hard day at the office.

Adopting a few good kitchen habits can make all the difference towards making the food you cook more wholesome so that the fuel you give your body can be in it's optimum restorative state.

- **Use very little or no oil**. Asian salad dressings rarely contain oil or vinegar and are usually made from lime juice, shallots and chilli.

- **Always store oils away from light** in tinted glass bottles or in refrigerator in order to protect them from oxidation which causes rancidity. Rancid oils promote internal chemical damage, so the fresher the oil the more healthful it is.

- **Trim all fat from meats**. Remove the skin from fish and poultry and chose only the least fatty cuts of meat.

- **Grill, poach, steam or bake** but avoid frying. If you must fry something, then deep-frying is preferable to shallow frying as the oil reaches a higher temperature; this allows for a shorter cooking time and the food can be successfully drained on a wire rack. If the food looks as if it needs to have excess oil removed with a paper towel, then you should not be considering eating it.

  Professional chefs love their deep-fryers, and whilst I have tried as much as possible to limit any frying in the following recipes, you will find a few exceptions, but these appear as optional garnishes. Younger or very active people can eat more fat than older or less active people, so you need to weigh up your own body's requirements before including more than moderate amounts of fried food into the diet.

- **Use a non-stick pan** to make oil less necessary. Substitute butter for vegetable oils as much as possible.

- **Avoid** the use of butter and cream when you can.

- **Don't be heavy-handed with salt**. Some Asian sauces such as fish sauce and soy sauce are laden with salt and should be seen as a salt alternative rather than a substitute. Soy sauce is a form of salt, but one which contains less sodium than table salt. As its flavour is stronger, one tends to use less. Natural soy sauces without preservatives are best, but be sure to refrigerate them. Some are even marked 'mild' or 'low sodium'.

- **Include a wide variety** of fresh fruits, vegetables, whole grain breads and cereals, legumes and pulses in your daily menu.

- **Don't over process** food by unnecessary peeling, de-seeding, pureeing or chopping ingredients too finely: eventually you will develop a taste for more textured food.

- **Vegetables** — Preserve the nutrients in vegetables by minimising cooking times. Don't allow them to soak in water or lounge around the bottom of the crisper for too long. Cut them up just before cooking or use them raw as much as you can. When boiling or steaming vegetables, try and re-use the water for stocks, gravies and soups.

Spa Cuisine is not about denial, but about controlling the balance.

Remember, daily care of your body from the inside is the best pampering of all — be good to yourself and eat wisely, because *you deserve it*.

Small changes can make big differences in the long run.

cook's notes

- **Teaspoon measures are 5ml.**
- **Tablespoons used in this book are those used in Europe and the US which measure 15 ml. Be sure to make allowance for this if using the 20 ml Australian measuring tablespoon.**
- **Liquid ingredients are given in metric volume measures; dry ingredients are weighed as this is the most accurate way to measure and will yield the most consistent results.**
- **Although it should go without saying, please read the recipe through in entirety before commencing to cook it.**

Unless otherwise indicated:

- **eggs are large,**
- **flour is all-purpose wheat flour**
- **black pepper is freshly ground,**
- **salt is ground sea salt,**
- **herbs are fresh,**
- **vegetable oil is sunflower or grapeseed,**
- **lime and lemon juices are freshly squeezed,**
- **and sugar is granulated.**

Cooking terms

brunoise – a very fine dice, approximately .5 cm.

butterfly – slit a piece of food in half horizontally, cutting it almost through so that when opened it resembles butterfly wings.

chiffonade – vegetable leaves, such as cabbage and lettuce, and large herbs, such as basil, are cut into fine shreds and used as garnish.

chinois – conical sieve made of perforated metal shaped like a chinaman's hat.

fond – stock formed from when water, bones, flavouring vegetables and seasonings have been slowly simmered. From the French literal translation, "the foundation."

garnish – refers in this book, to small amounts of a subsidiary ingredient of the dish, which are used to embellish the character and presentation of the completed dish.

julienne – to cut into thin, matchlike sticks.

nage – with connotations towards swimming, I guess this indirectly translates as a fancy name for a clear soup with things swimming in it.

pepperonata – a rustic Italian dish or style of dish of stewed peppers. There are innumerable variations on the theme.

prawns and shrimps – are regarded as interchangeable and the ingredients are named according to the particular chef's preference.

refresh – cool hot food quickly by plunging it into iced water, to stop it cooking.

saute – to cook and stir food, uncovered over medium heat.

sweat – to cook sliced or chopped food, usually vegetables in a tiny amount of fat and no liquid over low heat. Greaseproof paper or foil can be pressed on top so that the food steams in its own juices, usually before being added to other dishes.

the journey

Travel is a great educator and sometimes can be the vehicle we need to make a reality shift, to provide ourselves with the opportunity for personal change.

Whether it be to eliminate stress, gain inner strength, happiness or a sense of tranquillity, a sojourn in one of these spas can provide the perfect shift in perspective needed to create the setting for health and rejuvenation.

Once outside of our normal comfort zone, the senses are altered and immediately we can notice things that ordinarily escape our awareness.

Treatments available in the following spas are a journey in themselves – enabling you to enter a balanced world of earthly and spiritual perfections. The rejuvenating secrets of earthen clays, mountain botanicals, warming spices and cleansing water all come together to celebrate the healing power of nature.

So, when you find a huge gaping void in your work schedule, think of it in a positive light – this could be more than a good thing.

After all, the best moment for change in your entire life is now.

The destinations ...

four seasons resort maldives at kuda haraa

On the surface, The Maldives appears as *1200 tiny islands* comprising swaying palm trees amid endless stretches of *virgin white beaches*. Clustered in *26 coral atolls* in the Indian Ocean south-west of Sri Lanka, this *tropical republic* of islands (74 for tourist and 200 for Maldivians), is a much sought-after *diving and surfing* destination.

Don a mask and dive *into the blue*...

But venture beyond that spectacular infinity pool and you can avail yourself of the 35 dive sites within 10–60 minutes ride by *traditional dhoni*. When you do, you'll find yourself amidst the clearest waters you will ever encounter. Visibility up to 30 metres means the water is so clear you're tempted to breathe it.

Although you may not want to leave the island at all. *Create your own breeze* and borrow one of the cycles provided. *Sparkling azure waters* against cobalt blue skies stretch as far as the eye can see. And at night the ocean becomes a *mysterious mirror*, reflecting the lights of neighbouring islands and passing boats.

The simple fishing-based existence of the Maldivians ensures that the local diet is mainly seafood. Adjust the mask and snorkel and *hitch a ride on the tide*. Feed pieces of bread to the *abundant marine inhabitants* from your private deck. Thirty-eight thatched villas joined by a pier are suspended over a shallow lagoon, so that you can see fish swimming below. And for the land lovers, there are 68 beach front units.

Design influences from India and Morocco prevail, adding an authentic arabic flavour

*Most island resorts have their own spa.
At Kuda Huraa, the spa has its own island*

Black Pepper Basil Scrub

100 g fine table salt

30 g crushed black pepper

5 drops basil essential oil

1 tablespoon chopped basil leaves

squeeze of lemon

- Blend all ingredients together in a small bowl, adding a little water if necessary.
- Apply to wet skin and scrub the entire body, then rinse off. Moisturise as usual.

Lentil and Drumstick Leaf Soup

200 g yellow lentils, broken
100 g red lentils, broken
20 g whole garam masala*
25 ml vegetable oil
25 g ginger, crushed
50 g onion, sliced
50 g drumstick, roughly chopped
10 g mint sprigs
10 g ground turmeric
1 litre vegetable stock
20 g fresh drumstick leaves, blanched
20 ml lime juice
20 g scooped out inner seed and flesh of drumstick

- Wash the lentils well and boil in fresh water until they become a soft pulp. Save some for garnishing the soup. Heat the oil and sweat the garam masala and vegetables together until it they become aromatic.
- Add turmeric powder, sauté for few more minutes and add the mashed lentil and vegetable stock. Cook for a few minutes, then season with salt and pass it through a strainer.
- Heat again; add lime juice and the inner parts of the drumstick.
- Serve hot, garnished with boiled lentils.

*Whole garam masala:
Cinnamon stick, cloves, cardamom, pepper corn, cumin seeds, cinnamon leaves

Serves 4

Tomato Rasam

25 ml vegetable oil
50 g garlic, finely chopped
25 g ginger, finely chopped
15 g coriander seeds, crushed
5 g pepper corn, crushed
10 g cumin seeds, crushed
5 g ground chilli powder
5 g ground turmeric powder
pinch salt
25 g curry leaves with stem
50 g onion, sliced
500 g tomatoes, diced
1 litre water
50 g coriander leaf with stem
50 ml tamarind water*
12 tomato petals
5 g coriander leaves, chopped

- Heat oil and sweat the garlic, ginger, coriander seeds, pepper corn and cumin seeds untill light brown.
- Add the powdered spices and sauté for few seconds.
- Add the curry leaves and onion, sauté well, then add the tomatoes. Pour the water and let it boil, add coriander leaves and simmer until the water is well-flavoured.
- Add the tamarind water and season with salt. Pass it through a strainer, whisk it thoroughly to mash the tomatoes. Season with salt, garnish with chopped coriander and tomato petals.

*To make tamarind water see page 105:

Tomato petals:
Are slices of flesh from a peeled, firm tomato, sliced in a way to resemble rose petals.

Serves 4

Front to back: Lentil and Drumstick Leaf Soup, Tomato Rasam, Rice and Pickled Lime Broth

Rice and Pickled Lime Broth

1 litre rice stock
For rice stock, use the water which is drained off after cooking boiled red rice (see recipe below)
5 g fenugreek seeds
20 g pickled lime paste (preferably with red chilli)
40 g snake gourd, sliced
Salt

- Pour the rice stock into a pot and boil thoroughly with fenugreek seeds until they become soft.
- Strain and remove the seeds.
- Add the pickled lime paste and snake gourd to the stock and season with salt. Boil until the snake gourd is slightly softened.
- Serve hot.

Boiled Red Rice

400 g red rice
2 litres water

- Wash and soak the rice for 15 minutes.
- Boil the water, then add the rice to the water and boil until the rice is well cooked. Drain. Serve the rice hot.

Note:
To re-heat this rice, always use a steamer and steam it. The water which is drained off from the rice can be used as a stock for Rice and Pickled Lime Broth.

Serves 4

Tandoori Chicken with Pineapple Chaat

400 g chicken meat
60 ml Tandoori Red Masala
160 g pineapple, sliced
10 g coriander leaves, chopped
½ pineapple with the crown, flesh scooped out
40 pine nuts
60 ml Indian Cocktail Sauce
4 sprigs mint
10 g cumin, roasted and ground
salt

- Marinate the chicken meat in the Tandoori Red Masala for 1 hour. Bake in a hot oven for 20 minutes; leave to cool then slice into 5 cm strips.
- Mix chicken, pineapple, coriander and cocktail sauce together; toss it well. Season with salt, if necessary.
- Place the scooped out half pineapple with crown on a rattan place mat; arrange the salad inside.
- Scatter pinenuts on top, and garnish with mint sprig. Sprinkle roasted cumin seed on top.

Serves 3

Indian Cocktail Sauce
Equal quantity of plain yoghurt, Saffron Yoghurt, Tamarind Chutney, Raita.
- Season with Chaat Masala and roasted cumin powder.

Prawn and Kachumber Salad, with Honey Yoghurt Dressing

4 prawns, butterflied with tails on
pinch salt
4 crushed peppercorns
10 ml vegetable oil
10 g carrot, cut in julienne
10 g cucumber, cut in julienne
10 g beetroot, cut in julienne
5 g green bell pepper, cut in julienne
5 g red bell pepper, cut in julienne
10 g onion, sliced in rings
5 g coriander leaves, chopped
15 ml yoghurt
5 ml honey
2 g carom seeds, roasted and crushed
1 sprig of mint
2 lime wedges
1 copifai leaf

- Whisk together the yoghurt, honey and carom seeds; season with salt.
- In a bowl combine the carrot, cucumber, beetroot, bell peppers, onion and coriander.
- Marinate the prawns with salt, peppercorns and oil. Cook over a hot grill.
- Place the copifai leaf on the base of the plate. Pile the salad in the middle of the leaf, arranging the prawns around the base of the salad mound. Drizzle the dressing over the salad.
- Serve with lime wedges and sprig of mint.

Serves 1

Mango Lassi

400 ml thick yoghurt
400 ml skim milk
200 ml mango puree
20 ml rose water
5 g sugar (optional)

- Mix all the ingredients together and whisk well to bring out all the flavours.
- Keep refrigerated for one hour.
- Serve chilled.
- Garnish with a little granulated sugar on top

Masala Lassi

500 ml thick yoghurt	**5 g ginger, crushed**
500 ml skim milk	**5 g cumin seeds, roasted and crushed**
10 g coriander leaves, chopped	**salt**
1 green chilli, crushed	**chilled water**

- Mix all the ingredients together and whisk well to bring out all the flavours.
- If required, adjust the thickness of the yoghurt using water. Season with salt.
- Keep refrigerated for one hour.
- Strain well and serve chilled.
- Garnish with a little of the cumin seeds and chopped coriander, if desired.

Spinach and Citrus Salad

30 baby spinach leaves
10 g alfalfa sprouts
5 g enoki mushroom
6 orange segments
6 grape fruit segments
6 mandarin segments
6 lemon segments
6 lime segments
5 g green lentil sprouts
2 peppercorns, crushed
10 ml mustard oil
5 ml lime juice
salt
1 peppercorn, crushed

- Arrange the spinach leaves on the plate, making a circle. Place the citrus wedges one after the other between each leaf. Pile the alfalfa sprouts in the middle, and sprinkle the lentil sprouts on top.
- Arrange enoki mushrooms, one by one, on the salad. Using a pepper mill, season the salad with crushed pepper. Make the dressing by blending all the ingredients together. Spoon the dressing over the salad.

Serves 1

Banana and Coconut Foogath

600 g banana
200 g grated fresh coconut
5 g cumin seeds
5 g ground turmeric
2 green chillies
25 ml vegetable oil
5 g mustard seeds
100 g shallots, sliced
10 fresh curry leaves
water

- Peel the skin of the banana and dice it; keep in water to avoid colour change.
- Grind together coconut, green chilli, cumin and turmeric to a fine paste.
- Heat oil, and add the mustard seeds until they crackle, then add curry leaf and shallots. Sweat the shallots until well softened.
- Add the ground paste and banana; sprinkle with a little water and cover with a tight lid.
- Cook on a slow flame, stirring until the banana becomes soft. If it becomes too dry, sprinkle with more water to keep it moist.
- Serve hot with extra curry leaves to garnish.

Serves 4

Banana Trunk in Mild Spices

600 g banana trunk, cut in chunks
5 g ground turmeric
a little salt
25 ml vegetable oil
5 g cumin seed
10 g ginger, cut in julienne
10 g garlic, cut in julienne
100 g onion, sliced
5 g ground chilli
5 g ground coriander
100 g tomato, sliced
5 g coriander leaves, chopped

- Marinate the banana trunk with a little turmeric and salt; keep aside for few minutes. Heat oil, and add the cumin seed until it crackles. Add ginger, garlic and onion and cook until it becomes light brown. Mix the ground spices in water and add to the caramelised onion. Cook for a few minutes.
- Add the marinated banana trunk; cook for few seconds then add the tomato and salt. Cook over a slow flame until the banana becomes soft and the masala becomes dry and coats the banana. Add chopped coriander leaves and toss again.
- Serve hot, garnished with coriander leaf and diced tomato.

Serves 4

Front to back: Banana and Coconut Foogath, Banana Trunk in Mild Spices, Curried Yogurt and Plantain

Curried Yoghurt and Plantain

600 ml yoghurt
200 g coconut, freshly grated
5 g cumin seed
3 green chillies
10 g ginger
5 g ground turmeric
50 g medium ripe plantain, cut in thick discs
25 ml vegetable oil
5 g mustard seed
2 dried red chillies
10 curry leaves
50 g shallots, sliced
salt

- Whisk the yoghurt thoroughly; if too thick, add water to it to make it more smooth. Blend the coconut, cumin, green chilli, ginger and turmeric to a fine paste.
- Heat the oil, add mustard seeds, red chilli and curry leaf, and stir until crackling and fragrant. Add the shallots and cook until golden brown, then add the plantain and toss it through.
- Add the ground paste and simmer until the banana is cooked through.
- Pour in the beaten yoghurt, whisking until steaming. Do not allow the mixture to boil. Season with salt.
- If required add more water to make a smoother consistency. Serve warm or room temperature.

Serves 4

Spicy Yoghurt

800 ml Greek yoghurt
25 g ginger paste
50 g garlic paste
50 ml lime juice
100 ml mustard oil
20 g chaat masala
10 g ground cumin, roasted
5 g ground white pepper
10 g ajwain seeds, roasted and ground
10 g prepared mustard
salt

- Whisk all ingredients together until it becomes a thick smooth paste. Season with salt if required.
- Keep refrigerated.

Makes 1 litre

Uttapam is a kind of flat rice and lentil bread from Southern India. It is traditionally cooked on a tava, a round bronze hotplate, but any griddle or non-stick pan that you have at home will do.

More like a thick, round pancake, uttapam are usually eaten as a snack rather than to accompany a meal and can be studded with onions and chillies or other vegetables for variety.

Plain Uttapam

500 g raw rice

125 g white urad dhal

water

salt

For the Batter

- Wash the rice and dhal thoroughly until the water becomes clear. Leave to soak for one hour at room temperature.
- Grind to a fine paste using as little water as possible. Season with salt, and if required, add more water to make a pouring consistency. Keep at room temperature (30°C) for 6 hours, to allow the batter to ferment.
- After fermentation, mix it thoroughly and keep refrigerated.
- Heat the hot plate to 150°C. Clean thoroughly using oil, wiping clean with kitchen paper.
- Pour the batter onto the hotplate using a ladle. It will spread spontaneously and give equal thickness all over.
- When the underside is a golden colour, turn it over and cook the other side.
- Serve hot with Coconut Chutney.

Serves 4

Masala Uttapam

1 quantity Plain Uttapam

20 g onion, chopped

20 g tomato, chopped

5 g coriander leaves, chopped

5 g green chilli, chopped

- Prepare hotplate and pour on batter as in recipe for Plain Uttapam.
- When the batter has spread evenly over hotplate, sprinkle the topping of onion, tomato, coriander and chilli onto the uthappam while the batter is still uncooked. When the underside is a golden colour, turn it over and cook the other side.
- Serve hot with Coconut Chutney, presenting the side with vegetable visible.

Serves 4

Spiced Uttapam

1 quantity Plain Uttapam

5 g fried curry leaves

5 g fried mustard seeds

5 g fried red chilli flakes

- Prepare hotplate and pour on batter as in recipe for Plain Uttapam.
- When the batter has spread evenly over hotplate, sprinkle the topping of fried curry leaves, fried mustard seeds and fried red chilli onto the uthappam while the batter is still uncooked. When the underside is a golden colour, turn it over and cook the other side.

Serves 4

Carrot Uttapam

1 quantity Plain Uttapam

50 g carrot, boiled and chopped

- Prepare hotplate and pour on batter as in recipe for Plain Uttapam.
- When the batter has spread evenly over hotplate, sprinkle the carrots onto the uthappam while the batter is still uncooked. When the underside is a golden colour, turn it over and cook the other side.
- Serve hot with Coconut Chutney, presenting the side with carrot visible.

Serves 4

Coconut Chutney

1 coconut, grated	**salt**
5 g green chilli	**10 ml vegetable oil**
5 g ginger	**5 g mustard seeds**
5 g coriander leaf	**3 dried red chillies**
1 lime, juice only	**5 curry leaves**

- Mix the ingredients for grinding together in a blender with enough water to cover the ingredients. Make a fine paste, season with salt.
- Heat oil and saute the mustard seeds, red chilli and curry leaves until they crackle.
  While it is very hot, pour to the chutney base and mix immediately Adding the paste to the hot oil ensures the flavour is well infused.
- Serve hot or cold.

Steamed Plantain with Palm Honey

8 South Indian long plantain, ripe
100 ml palm sugar syrup
20 g grated fresh coconut

- Trim the edges of the plantain, and arrange it in a steamer.
- Cover with a tight lid and steam until the fruit becomes soft and well cooked.
- Place it on a serving plate with banana leaf, open the skin a little, and sprinkle with some freshly grated coconut.
- Serve hot with palm sugar syrup on the side.

Serves 4

Palm Sugar Syrup

500 g palm sugar
250 ml water

- Melt the palm sugar in water in a small saucepan over low heat.
- Cool the syrup, strain, then pour into sterilised jars.
- Store in the refrigerator until required.

Saffron Yoghurt

0.5g saffron
50 ml water
1 litre thick yoghurt
salt to taste

- Boil the saffron with water and reduce to 10 ml. Pour this to the yoghurt and add salt. Whisk thoroughly until it becomes smooth and the colour is evenly dispersed. Keep refrigerated.

Tamarind Chutney

800 g tamarind, seeds removed
30 g ginger, minced
30 g garlic, minced
5 dried red chillies
10 g whole garam masala, see page 25
10 g Chaat Masala
5 g ground turmeric
200 g jaggery
10 g cumin seeds, roasted and crushed
salt

- In a saucepan, place the tamarind, ginger, garlic, chilli, garam masala, chaat masala and turmeric and add enough water to cover.
- Bring to the boil then reduce heat and simmer until the tamarind is very soft, adding a little more water as required, to prevent it from catching. Strain the mixture, discarding the lumps. Add jaggery and continue to cook over a slow flame, until chutney is reduced to a pouring consistency. Pass through strainer once again.
- Season with salt, keep refrigerated.

Raita (Mint Yoghurt)

500 ml thick yoghurt
100 g mint leaves, shredded

- Combine the yoghurt and mint leaves together. Season with salt.
- Keep covered in refrigerator until required.

Chaat Masala

1 tablespoon cumin seeds, toasted and ground
1 tablespoon ground coriander
1½ tablespoons ground amchur
1 tablespoon ground chilli
1 teaspoon ground white pepper
1 teaspoon black salt
1 teaspoon salt

- Combine all ingredients together and store in a sealed jar, until required.

Onion and Beetroot Akchar

100 g onion, in thick slices
100 g beetroot, cut in batons
200 ml white vinegar
100 g sugar

- Dissolve the sugar in the vinegar. Add the onion and beetroot and stir until completely coated. Refrigerated overnight.
- Drain the liquid; serve chilled.

The simple fishing-based existence of the Maldivians ensures that the local diet is mainly seafood.

The simple fishing-based existence of the Maldivians ensures that the local diet is mainly seafood.

Maharaja Kebabs

3 or 4 pcs Lobster Kebab

3 or 4 pcs Lamb Sheesh Kebab

3 or 4 pcs Ajwaini Tuna Tikka

50 g Onion and Beetroot Akchar

- Spoon some of the Onion and Beetroot Akchar onto a banana leaf at the base of the skewer stand.
- Arrange 4 pieces of lamb, fish and lobster separately on 3 different skewers. Hang the kebabs on the skewer stand and serve immediately.

Chaat Dressing

250 ml yoghurt

250 ml Saffron Yoghurt

250 ml Mint Yoghurt

250 ml Tamarind Chutney

15 g coriander, chopped

20 g cumin seeds, roasted and crushed

20 g Chaat Masala

- Mix all the ingredients together and whisk thoroughly.
- Check the seasoning, and keep refrigerated.

Sheesh Kebabs

500 g minced lamb, fairly lean
25 g ginger
25 g garlic
10 g green chilli
10 g mint leaves
10 g coriander leaves
5 g cumin seeds, roasted
5 g garam masala
5 g ground fenugreek leaves
50 g amul cheese, grated
5 g cardamom seeds, crushed
10 g Chaat Masala

- Mince all the ingredients together thoroughly in a meat mincer. Season with salt, and using the hand mix and beat well to make it soft. Pack it around the tandoori skewer, in a long cylindrical shape. Heat oven to highest setting.
- Bake in a hot oven for 8 minutes. Do not over cook or the meat will dry out. Sprinkle with chaat masala and serve it on the skewer.

Lobster Kebabs

960 g lobster medallions, 16 x 60 g portions
5 g ginger garlic paste
5 g ground chilli
2 g ground turmeric
3 g garam masala
5 g grain mustard
50 ml Tandoori Red Masala
10 ml lime juice
5 g Chaat Masala
5 g coriander leaves, chopped

- Marinate the lobster with ginger garlic paste, chilli, turmeric, garam masala and mustard. Apply the tandoori red masala to the lobster and keep in the refrigerator for one hour.
- Heat oven to highest setting. Bake in a hot oven on a metal skewer for 7 minutes. Sprinkle with lime juice, chaat masala and chopped coriander leaves on top and serve hot.

Ajwaini Tuna Tikka

960 g tuna, cut in 16 cubes x 60 g
200 ml Chaat Dressing
10 g ginger garlic paste
5 ml lime juice
10 ml saffron water
5 g ajwain seeds, roasted and cracked
5 g Chaat Masala
5 ml lime juice
5 g coriander leaves, chopped
salt

- Rub ginger garlic paste, lime juice and salt on the fish cubes. Mix saffron water with Chaat Dressing and whisk well until it turns yellow. Add ajwain seeds to the masala and mix well. Baste the fish cubes with the yellow masala paste and keep refrigerate for one hour.
- Heat oven to highest setting. Bake in a hot oven on a metal skewer for 6 minutes. Sprinkle with chaat masala, lime juice, and chopped coriander leaves on top and serve hot.

Fresh Coconut Milk

300 g freshly grated coconut
300 ml luke warm water

- Coarsely blend the water and coconut together. Using a fine strainer, separate the milk and the coconut.
- Discard the coconut after squeezing the milk from it.

Tandoori Reef Fish

1 whole white snapper, about 700 g, cleaned
60 ml Tandoori Red Masala
10 g ginger garlic paste
5 g lime juice
5 ml lime juice
5 g chaat masala
5 g coriander leaves, chopped
salt

- Combine the ginger garlic paste, lime juice and salt and rub it onto the fish. Baste the Tandoori Red Masala on the fish and keep in the fridge for one hour.
- Bake in a hot oven on a metal skewer for 20 minutes.
- Sprinkle with lime juice, Chaat Masala and chopped coriander leaves on top and serve hot.

Serves 2

Tandoori Red Masala

100 ml Chaat Dressing
5 g Kashmiri red chilli
5 ml mustard oil
salt

- Boil the dry red chilli in water and mustard oil until it becomes soft and well cooked. Strain off the liquid and blend the chilli to a fine paste. Add the Chaat Dressing and combine well. Season with salt if necessary.

* See glossary

hotel intercontinental hong kong

The more times you visit Hong Kong, the harder it becomes to keep away.

As it continues to *evolve*, this city is still, and always will be, *exciting and exotic*; hectic, steamy, and *quirky* as ever. The harbour, the Peak, endless *oriental curiosities* and *edgy galleries* all beckon at once, drawing you amidst the *heady aromas* in the streets heaving with human traffic.

The spa at the Hotel Inter-Continental Hong Kong incorporates the *ancient philosophy* of *feng shui* to create balance and well-being in one's life and environment. Feng Shui aims to achieve the *perfect symmetry* between the yin and the yang by utilising the five basic elements of water, wood, fire, earth and metal, which when in harmony *create free-flowing life energy*, or ch'i. Metal sculptures, traditional Chinese fish bowls, flowing water and relaxation chimes are all a part of this *Oriental art* which has been practiced for almost *4000 years* to improve health, wealth, career and relationships.

With a little basic knowledge of which foods affect *your body type*, and the ways in which they affect it, the *yin and yang* eventually becomes *intuitive* and you can form an understanding of how to *avoid diseases* which are consistent with your physical type.

Water, one of the five elements of Fengshui, balances out the inner and outer world

For centuries, Traditional Chinese Medicine has been the mainstay of healthcare for a quarter of the world's population, and during that time, it's methods have changed very little.

Drawing on different philosophies than Western Medicine, TCM has a different way of looking at how the body works and of diagnosing illness; looking at the big picture rather than narrowing the illness down to one part of the body. A practitioner may listen to the strength of voice, assess a persons smell, colour of urine, level of thirst, and check the pulse in both wrists in order diagnose a condition. The state of a patients *chi*, or life energy, is also assessed, as blockage or deficiency is believed to cause disease. And to make it even more intriguing, the treatment, which often includes acupuncture, herbal and dietary adjustments, is customised so that a practitioner may treat four different patients with the same condition in four completely different ways. Curiously, the pins versus pills approach is rapidly gaining favour with Western doctors.

The *yin* and *yang* comes into play in food by using the healing properties of ordinary ingredients and by understanding their flavours, energies, actions and movements. Once your body type has been assessed, either hot, cold, dry or damp, disposition and sex drive, and your "*y-score*" is determined, a practitioner can develop your own personalised approach to disease *prevention* and health.

Home-made Yoghurt

500 ml milk

some active-culture yoghurt

- Bring milk just to the boil and leave to cool to 38–46°C, measuring on a dairy thermometer.
- Outside this temperature the bacteria are inactive.
- Whisk in some active-culture yoghurt, pour into two 250 ml jars and cover. Keep the mixture warm at 24–29°C by wrapping in a towel for 6–8 hours, or in a gas oven with the pilot light on.

Note
- An electric yoghurt maker can be used, these maintain a constant temperature which produces a more consistent texture than the above method.
- When the yoghurt has set, stir in any desired flavourings such as fruit puree, and refrigerate for 12 hours before serving. Fruit puree can be sweetened before adding to yoghurt, if desired.

Sugar Pea Soup with Truffle Foam

Soup:
500 g sugar peas
100 g chopped onion
2 litres chicken stock
200 ml light cream
salt and pepper to taste
15 ml extra virgin olive oil

Foam:
500 ml milk, warmed
a little truffle oil

- Sweat the onion and sugar peas in a non-stick pan with a little oil. Add chicken stock and cook until sugar peas are soft. Place in blender with cream and salt and pepper.
- Blend until smooth then seive through a fine strainer.
- Add a little truffle oil to warm milk and, using a hand mixer, whisk until it becomes foaming.
- Pour soup into serving glasses and top with truffle foam.

Lobster with Green Apple and Avocado

1.4 kg Boston lobster tail, shell removed

2 avocadoes, firm but ripe, roughly chopped

2 green apples, 5cm dice

4 tablespoons wasabi paste

20 ml Tabasco

4 small red chilli

40 g coriander, finely chopped

2 limes, juice only

100 g semi-dried tomatoes, in 5cm dice

240 g salad mix (frisee, butter lettuce, coral or lambs)

60 ml Vanilla Balsamic Reduction (see page 45)

80 ml Citrus Vinaigrette

Citrus Vinaigrette:

Combine 1 tablespoon lime juice, 1 tablespoon white wine vinegar with 3 tablespoons olive oil. Season to taste.

- Marinate the lobster portions in a little Citrus Vinaigrette and leave aside.
- In a bowl, gently combine chopped avocado, green apple, wasabi paste, coriander, Tabasco, chopped chilli, lime juice, and season to taste.
- Place an egg ring on a serving plate and spoon some chopped tomato to cover the base of the ring. Cover with a layer of avocado, then carefully remove ring.
- Place the lobster tail carefully on the avocado to follow the shape of the circle. Toss the salad mix in some of the remaining Citrus Vinaigrette and place decoratively on top of lobster.
- Place droplets of Vanilla Balsamic Reduction in an arc on the plate around the lobster.

Serves 4

Cajun Tuna Loin with Tomato Confit

120 g potato

30 ml whipping cream

pinch nutmeg

320 g baby carrots

240 g green asparagus

240 g broccoli

240 g cauliflower

4 x 180 g tuna fillets, bones removed

5 g cajun spice mix

120 g salad mix

Tequila Vinaigrette:

3 tablespoons Vanilla Balsamic Reduction (see page 45)

20 ml Tequila

80 g yellow cherry tomatoes

80 g red cherry tomato

- Boil potatoes until soft, remove skins and mix with cream, nutmeg and season to taste.
- Steam the baby carrots, green asparagus, broccoli and cauliflower until just tender, and keep warm at 80ºC until required.
- Coat the tuna fillet in the cajun spice mix
- Pan-fry the tuna fillets in a dry non-stick pan over medium heat.
- Place mashed potato into centre of plate with a little salad on top.
- Spoon vegetables around the mound.
- Slice tuna on an angle in 1.5cm thickness, and arrange around the mound.
- Scatter with some cherry tomatoes and drizzle with Tequilla Vinaigrette.

Serves 4

Mille-feuille of Crab

Semi Dried Tomato Salsa:
45 g semi dried tomato
15 ml walnut oil
15 ml sherry vinegar
salt and pepper to taste

Avocado Compote:
half avocado
quarter Fuji apple
juice of ½ lemon

Mango Salad:
40 g mango,
cut in small diced
25 g red onion,
finely chopped
20 g red chilli,
finely chopped
20 g coriander,
finely chopped

Crab Meat:
60 g crab meat
10 g chives
15 g mayonnaise

Herb Salads:
20 g mixed salad leaves
10 g chervil

- Blend together semi-dried tomatoes with walnut oil, sherry vinegar until smooth. Season with salt and pepper to taste.
- Finely dice the avocado and Fuji apple and coat in the lemon juice to avoid discolouration. Mix together and press them into a ring mold in the centre of a serving plate.
- Combine the mango salad ingredients and place on top of the avocado compote.
- Mix crabmeat with mayonnaise and chives and spoon mixture on top of the mango salad.
- Garnish with a little salad and chervil on top. Draw a line of semi-dried tomato salsa on plate along side the mille-feuille.

Serves 1

Seared King Prawn with Gazpacho Salad

4 king prawns
1 g Cajun Spice Mix
(available in supermarkets)

Gazpacho:
375 g tomato
175 g cucumber
40 g red bell pepper
1 clove garlic, peeled

250 ml chicken stock
12 g tomato paste
50 g ketchup
salt and pepper to taste
lemon juice to taste
20 g mixed salad leaves
1 stalk lemongrass

- Coat the prawns in the Cajun Spice Mix and sear in a non-stick pan for 1-2 minutes, until cooked.

For the Gazpacho

- Blend all ingredients with chicken stock and season to taste.
- Sieve with fine strainer.
- Pour a little gazpacho into the base of each serving bowl.
- Arrange salad leaves on top of the gazpacho.
- Place a prawn across the top of each salad, and garnish with lemongrass.

Serves 4

Crispy Skin Red Snapper in Bouillabaisse

4 x 320 g red snapper fillet
12 Shrimp Shomai
1 kg spinach
1 litre Bouillabaise
1 bunch dill
600 g assorted shellfish (peeled prawns, mussels in shell, clams in shell)

- Saute spinach in garlic olive oil, season with nutmeg, salt and pepper, and keep warm at 80°C until serving.
- Lightly brush the base of a heavy-based pan with grape seed oil. When the pan is hot, fry the fish, skin-side down, until golden and crispy.
- Place steamed shrimp shomai and sauteed spinach onto a serving plate.
- Spoon the poached seafood around the fish with a little of the Bouillabaisse and garnish with dill.

Serves 4

Shrimp Shomai

240 g peeled shrimp	**sugar**
12 wonton skins	**vegetable oil**
120 g lean pork mince	**sesame oil**
1 tablespoon cornflour	**ground white pepper**
salt	**coriander**

- Finely chop the shrimp and toss into a bowl containing the minced pork.
- Add in the other ingredients, excluding wonton skins, and quickly combine until all is incorporated.
- Working with 3-4 wonton skins at a time, place about 1 tablespoon of the mixture onto each wonton skin. Shape to form a dumpling. Continue with remaining filling and wonton skins. Spoon flying fish roe on top.
- Steam for about 5 minutes.

Makes 12

Bouillabaisse

150 ml fish stock	**3 g saffron strands**
10 g onion	**¼ lemon, juice only**
10 g leek	**½ tablespoon Pernod**
10 g tomato, chopped	**50 g prawns, peeled**
15 g fennel	**50 g red snapper fillet**
2 cloves garlic	**100 g clams**
8 g parsley	**100 g mussels**
½ orange, zest only	

- Reduce fish stock with all the ingredients, excluding seafood. Poach the seafood in the Bouillabaisse for 2 minutes, just prior to serving.

Poached Chicken Roulade with Forest Mushroom Ragout

240 g snow pea sprouts
240 g bean sprouts
240 g shiitake mushroom
30 ml olive oil
salt and pepper to taste
850 g chicken breast
200 g baby potatoes
240 g shallots
40 ml red wine
1 teaspoon sugar
360 g leaf spinach, well washed and drained
240 g red bell pepper
1 bunch chervil
80 ml Demi-Glace (see recipe page 128)

- Saute snow pea sprouts, beansprouts and mushrooms in olive oil with salt and pepper.
- Place each chicken breast between two pieces of plastic wrap, and gently pound the flesh with a mallet, to flatten slightly. Lay them out on a board and divide the mushroom and sprout mixture between them. Roll them up and wrap in kitchen wrap, securing the edges well.
- Poach chicken roulade in simmering water for about 6-8 minutes, remove from water and keep aside. slice and place on top of vegetables.
- Place pan-fried potatoes and caramelised shallots, on the side of the chicken. Serve with a little Demi-Glace sauce.

Ahi Tuna Loin Roll Filled with Crabmeat

Vanilla Balsamic Reduction:
600 ml balsamic vinegar
1 vanilla bean
40 g birds eye chilli

Wasabi Apple Vinaigrette:
1 litre plain yoghurt
600 ml apple juice, reduced to 100 ml
10 g wasabi powder
1 lemon, juice only

1 globe artichoke
240 g crabmeat
½ cup yoghurt
salt and pepper to taste
1 lemon, juice only
small bunch chives, finely chopped
480 g portion Ahi tuna
200 g mixed salad greens

For the Vanilla Balsamic Reduction
- Reduce the Balsamic vinegar with the vanilla bean and chilli until a light syrup. Strain and store in refrigerator until required. Makes 300 ml.

For the Wasabi Apple Vinaigrette
- In a bowl combine the yoghurt, apple juice reduction, wasabi and lemon juice to make a smooth dressing. Makes 1.5 litres.

- Cut artichoke vertically into thin slices, and place them in acidulated water until ready to use. Drain artichoke slices and dry with paper towel. Spread them on a lightly oiled baking tray and dry out in a low oven for about 40 minutes.
- Combine the crabmeat with yoghurt, salt, pepper, lemon juice and chive to taste. Slice the tuna thinly to get 4 slices, 10 cm x 6 cm. Place the prepared crabmeat salad in the centre and roll it up. Wrap in cling wrap and chill for at least 10 minutes.
- Brush the plate with Balsamic Reduction. Place tuna roll on the plate and garnish with salad greens, artichokes crisps and Wasabi Apple Vinaigrette.

Wild Mango Sorbet and Fresh Tropical Fruit on Ice

160 g Mango Sorbet
720 g mango
600 g honey dew melon
600 g cantaloupe flesh
50 g dragon fruit
100 g strawberries
240 g plums
120 g cherries
40 g small star fruit

For the Mango Sorbet:
1 kg mango puree
¼ cup honey
1 cup caster sugar
pinch salt

- Combine the mango puree, honey, sugar and salt in the bowl of an ice-cream machine bowl. Churn according to machine's instructions and keep in freezer until required.
- Cut mango, honey melon, cantaloupe and dragon fruit into 2 cm dice.
- Wash remaining fruit.
- Hull the strawberries. Remove stones from plums and slice into eigths. Remove stems and stones from cherries. Slice star fruit in .5 cm thickness.
- Gently toss all fruit in a bowl and serve with scoops of Mango Sorbet.

ana mandara resort
nha trang, vietnam

After sampling the *colourful* and *frenetic display* of cuisine, commerce and culture Vietnam offers, you might find yourself seeking a *"chill out"* destination.

We found one.... Situated on the whitest of white sand beaches, furnished with *native woods* and *rattan*, the Ana Mandara Resort, Nha Trang is enchantingly reminiscent of an old Vietnamese village.

Lotus flowers are everywhere, reflecting the image of purity and spirituality. On arrival we are offered *lotus tea*, enjoyed both for its romantic powers and its sweet aroma.

An early morning market tour with the chef, *en cyclo*, takes you along *Tan Phu* Boulevard, which, far from being a contrived tourist *"theatre"* as it may appear, is all a part of quotidian life.

Fragrant smells, redolent of Asia, waft from sparkling windows, hung with glistening whole barbecued ducks.

Baguettes stacked on bicycle racks – still a favourite in this *post-colonial enclave*, hinting of former influences.

Local children instinctively posing for photographs.

Flower sellers bicycles straining under the weight and imbalance of their *exotic loads*.

Chinese vendors frantically sorting, counting and proudly rearranging their stock.

Chefs wielding flashing cleavers, chop frantically while packing take-home containers of their *delicious treats*.

Sand Aerobics increases intensity of the exercise. Begin slowly to build up balance – start with walking lunges.

Baby Massage

Massage is a natural extension of cuddling and playing with your baby, so take time out to share a few special moments. After a bath is usually an ideal time for baby, when he is warm relaxed and calm. Be sure the room temperature is a warm 26ºC, and allow adequate time. Make sure you allow adequate time so you don't need to rush. If the baby is not in the mood… simply try again later.

- Touch your babies skin gently by using in little strokes, using fingertips and thumbs for small areas and the palm of your hand to softly move the muscles under the skin in larger areas. Close your eyes and press your eyelids. To judge the amount of pressure required, close your eyes and press firmly on your eyelids without causing any discomfort.

- Massage should flow from head to toes, starting at the head then to the face shoulders, arms, chest, stomach then legs. Talk to baby in soothing tones and make constant eye contact to establish a more visual and tactile communication.

- A foot massage is very relaxing and can sometimes help reduce stomach pain. Begin by putting a soft pressure on each toe, then the foot and return to the toes again. Gently caress all the toes, applying circular movements at the heels.

- Best oil to use is a light vegetable oil such as sweet almond or sunflower oil.

On the chef's recommendation, we start the day with a thick fruit shake or soursop juice over crushed ice.

A breakfast "must have" is the beef pho (see recipe on page 58), washed down with a Da Nang coffee, made from freshly roasted and ground Vietnamese coffee, filtered through a special drip-through gadget, and blended with condensed milk – a constant in Vietnamese cuisine.

Cho dam market

Ginger Tea

2 g dried ginger

7 g fresh ginger

4 g dried orange peel

2 cups boiling water

brown sugar to taste

· Boil gingers, orange peel and water together for 3 minutes. Pour in teapot and serve, strained.

Note
Ginger is used daily by over half the world's population. As a "yang" food, its warming and stimulating properties are said to prevent the body from becoming too damp. As it calms and purifies, it counter-balances the cooling "yin" foods to create harmony in the body.

Prawn Congee

1 litre fish stock
¼ teaspoon salt
100 g rice
½ cup water
300 g prawn meat, chopped into bite-size pieces
15 ml sesame oil
15 ml nuoc mam
15 ml soy
20 g scallions, roughly chopped
20 g Vietnamese mint
20 g coriander

- Bring fish stock to the boil, add salt, then add rice, stirring gently until it returns to the boil.
- Lower heat and simmer, uncovered, for 1 hour, stirring occasionally. After 20 minutes, add water. Most of the liquid will have evaporated towards the end of the cooking time, so take care to stir rice more regularly to avoid the porridge catching on the bottom of the pot.
- Combine half of the soy, nuoc mam and sesame oil and sprinkle over the prawn meat.
- When porridge has reached the desired texture, remove from heat.
- Stir the prawn meat into the hot rice porridge and stir until prawns are pink and cooked through, about 2 minutes.
- Spoon congee into small bowls and drizzle remaining soy and sesame mix over top. Garnish with spring onions, mint and coriander leaves or serve separately in bowls.

Serves 2

Beef Pho

1 litre beef stock, simmering
100 g banh pho, rice noodles
2 handfuls mung bean sprouts, roots removed
80 g beef fillet, sliced
40 g scallions, finely sliced
40 g lettuce leaves, chiffonade
3 g salt
3 ml nuoc mam
10 ml soy sauce
mint sprigs
chopped coriander
sliced chillies
lime wedges

- Soak banh pho in warm water for 30 minutes; drain. Add nuoc mam and soy to simmering stock.
- Place a serving of noodles in each bowl and top with a handful of mung bean sprouts.
- In a large ladle, place some slices äof beef and spring onions. Dip ladle into boiling soup and pour over noodles, adding more soup to each bowl. Serve immediately with a side plate of mint chilli and coriander.

Serves 2

Beef Stock

1 kg beef bones
500 g gravy beef
1 brown onion
6 cloves
10 black peppercorns
2.5 cm ginger
1 cinnamon stick
3 star anise
5 cardamom pods
2 carrots
1 sprig celery leaves
30 ml nuoc mam

- Cut onion into quarters, leaving skin on, and place in a stock pot with remaining ingredients. Cover with cold water, about 3 litres.
- Bring to the boil, then simmer for 3 hours, skimming the surface several times.
- Add salt to taste, then strain, and set aside until required.

Salad of Julienned Vegetable

100 g carrot

100 g snow pea

100 g cabbage

100 g cucumber

100 g tomato

100 g scallions

100 g capsicum

100 g mango

100 g red cabbage

10 g salt

3 g freshly ground black pepper

20 ml peanut oil

1 tablespoon sesame oil

juice of 2 limes

1 tablespoon nuoc mam

2 tablespoons chopped mint

20 g roasted unsalted peanuts, roughly chopped

handful coriander sprigs

- Finely slice all the vegetables into thin strips.
- Combine salt, black pepper, peanut oil, sesame oil, lime juice and nuoc mam in a small bowl.
- Place all the shredded vegetables into a mixing bowl. Drizzle the sauce over the mixture and toss well to combine.
- Transfer the salad onto serving plates. Sprinkle the mint and chopped nuts, then garnish with coriander sprigs.

Seafood Omelette with Bean Sprouts

Tomato filling:

100 g tomato

10 g onion

5 g garlic

200 g peeled prawns

200 g sea bass, garfish or snapper

20 ml balsamic vinegar

10 g Vietnamese basil, chopped

10 g coriander, chopped

Omelette:

6 eggs

1 tablespoon water

20 g enoki mushrooms

4 handfuls bean sprouts

finely sliced chillies

- Chop the tomato, onion and garlic, and sweat them together in a pan with a little vegetable oil over low heat. Cook until the onion is soft and transparent and the mixture is quite dry. Gently stir the seafood through the mixture until prawns are pink and fish is just cooked, about 2 minutes. Season with balsamic vinegar and herbs. Set aside.
- Whisk eggs with water for 30 seconds until frothy.
- Heat a non-stick pan which has been brushed with a little vegetable oil, and when hot, pour half of the mixture into the pan. Cook until the edges begin to brown. Spoon half of the seafood tomato mixture over one side of the omelette. Sprinkle with half of the mushrooms, bean shoots and chilli.
- Fold omelette over and continue cooking for another minute. Remove onto serving plate. Repeat steps 2-4 with remaining ingredients to make another omelette.
- Garnish with some coriander or mint and serve hot with a small bowl of soy sauce on the side. The omelette can also be served with plain rice.

Serves 2

Seafood Hot Pot

2 litres fish stock
100 g garlic
2 large onions
300 g carrot, cut in 6mm slices
200 g ginger
100 g chilli
100 g lemongrass
50 g salt
100 g sugar
pinch cayenne pepper
200 g prawns
200 g squid
200 g groper, cut in 3cm cubes
400 g clams
400 g scallops
300 g chinese cabbage, cut in 5cm squares
8 fresh shiitake mushrooms, stems removed
800 g cooked egg noodles
300 g mustard leaf
100 g chives, finely chopped
30 ml light soy sauce

- Soak clams for 5 minutes in a solution of 1 lt of cold water mixed with 2 tablespoons of salt. Rinse under cold running water and drain.
- Peel prawns, leaving tail attached. Remove vein by inserting a wooden skewer under vein and lifting it up.
- Score a cross in the top of each mushroom with the tip of a sharp knife.
- Blanch carrot in boiling water for 1 minute, then drain and refresh them in cold water.
- Heat fish stock in a flameproof casserole at the table. Add garlic, onions, carrots, ginger, chilli, salt, sugar and cayenne pepper. Cook remaining ingredients in about 4 batches. Take a little of each of the, fish, shellfish, noodles and vegetables.
- Maintaining a steady simmer, remove the items as they cook or allow diners to serve themselves. Replenish the casserole with remaining food items as required.
- To serve, pour soy sauce into small individual dipping bowls and mix chives into it.

Serves 4

Goi Cuon

800 g prawns, steamed and peeled with tails removed
200 g lettuce, chiffonade
60 g bean sprouts
100 g selection of fresh basil, mint and coriander leaves
100 g rice vermicelli
50 g shallots, finely chopped
50 g chive
200 g boneless pork, boiled and thinly sliced
8 dried rice papers
satay sauce (see recipe page 61)
Nuoc Cham for dipping
50 g peanuts, finely chopped

- Boil the rice vermicelli quickly in water, rinse in cold water and drain.
- Soften the rice papers, one or two at a time, in a bowl of hand-hot water. When softened, about 8–10 seconds, remove papers from the water and drain on a kitchen towel.
- Place a little of each ingredient on the softened rice paper and start to roll up firmly, folding in the sides towards the centre.
- Before completely rolled, tuck a chive stem along the fold line leaving a portion of the stem to poke out of the roll.
- Serve with extra herbs and lettuce leaves. Pour dipping sauces into small bowls and sprinkle peanuts on top. Dip the rolls in the sauce as you eat.

Makes 8 rolls

Note: These rolls can be prepared a few hours in advance, kept covered with a damp towel or plastic wrap and kept at room temperature until required.

Nuoc Cham

- In a mortar and pestle, grind 2 cloves of garlic, 1 small red chilli and 2 tablespoons sugar.
- Stir in 2 tablespoons lime juice, ¼ cup rice vinegar and ¼ cup nuoc mam; serve as dipping sauce.

Mango, Pineapple and Orange Cooler

200 g mango
200 g pineapple
200 ml orange juice
30 g ice
5 g honey

- Peel mango and pineapple and blend with orange juice ice and honey.
- Pour into a chilled serving glass and garnish with lime.

Watermelon and Fennel Quencher

600 g watermelon flesh
5 g fennel seed
30 g ice
5 g honey

- Peel fruit and blend with fennel, ice and honey.
- Strain and pour into chilled serving glass. Garnish with a slice of watermelon rind.

Lemongrass Tea

60 g lemongrass
60 g ginger
20 g green tea
2 litres boiling water
20 g sea weed, such as hijiki, or konbu

- Place lemongrass, ginger and green tea into a jug and pour the boiling water over. Leave to infuse for 2 minutes.
- Add seaweed and leave to infuse for a further minute. Strain and serve immediately. Garnish with a slice of lemon. Can also be chilled and stored to serve later as Iced Lemongrass Tea.

Mango with Chilli and salt

2 large mangoes, well chilled
15g salt
15g ground chilli

- Combine salt and chilli powder together.
- Peel mangoes, remove stone and cut into large chunks.
- Place mango chunks on serving plate and make a line of chilli-salt. Serve immediately.

Serves 2

Satay Sauce

2 cloves garlic
3 tablespoons sugar
1 large red chilli, roughly chopped
½ cup ground peanuts
½ cup crunchy peanut butter
½ cup hoisin
½ cup lemon juice
1 cup water

- In a mortar and pestle, grind together garlic, sugar, chilli and peanuts until smooth.
- Stir in peanut butter, then one by one add hoisin sauce, lemon juice and enough water to make a dipping consistency.

chiva som
hua hin, thailand

Just a short distance from the *King's summer palace* in the town of Hua Hin is the dedicated health resort of Chiva Som, providing a *controlled environment* where actual health benefits can be gained.

This is a place for grown-ups without toys or bad habits. Children under the age of 16 are not allowed, neither are mobile phones, and wines and champagne are available, but only in the evenings.

Practitioners are on hand to advise on *western and alternative medicine*, nutrition, exercise and fitness. The mantra is to achieve *maximum results* by working with the body and the mind, *educating guests* to assist them in continuing the benefits on return home.

Start the day with an energising stretch class or Tai Chi in one of the outdoor pavilions and end it with a power *walk on the beach*. Throughout the day a variety of classes are provided in the air-conditioned *dance studios*. Programmes as diverse as *lifestyle planning*, personal image and *stress management* are available.

The first rule at Chiva Som is to forget the notion that *diet* and *nutrition* equate to uninspiring food; the calorie-counted cookery classes available help guests to embrace that concept and take the *knowledge* away with them. The Chiva Som team of Thai and international chefs prepare the ever-changing daily fare, using produce from the resort's *own garden*. No matter how long you stay, the food is never boring.

Warm-stone massage

Smooth, warmed rocks glide across your body in long, flowing strokes, while other warm stones are placed on various energy points to encourage the healing potential. A soothing muscle-melt.

Floating on water with the same salinity and density as that of the Dead Sea creates a sense of weightlessness and isolation, providing a deep feeling of relaxation and sensory awareness. Half an hour in this tank is said to give the restorative benefits of 2 hours' sleep.

Cleansing Cocktail

200 g cucumber
200 g carrot
200 g apple
100 g beetroot
2½ cm ginger

- Place all ingredients in a blender and blitz until smooth. Serve with a slice of lemon.

Fresh Complexion

400 g pineapple, flesh only
200 g cucumber
200 g green apple

- Place all ingredients in a blender and blitz until smooth.
- Serve with a slice of green apple.

Germ Warfare

240 ml orange juice
30 ml lemon juice
200 g carrot
1 clove garlic

- Pass carrot and garlic through a juicing machine, then blend with the citrus juices. Serve with a slice of carrot.

Pomelo and Prawn Salad

150 g pomelo flesh
60 ml lemon juice
15 ml soy sauce
30 ml honey
1 clove garlic, crushed
5 small red chillies, finely sliced
10 g scallions, finely sliced
1 stalk lemongrass, trimmed and sliced thinly
30 g shallots, finely chopped
1 tablespoon toasted coconut flakes
1 teaspoon toasted almonds
200 g green prawns, poached then peeled
10 g coriander

- Break the pomelo segments into 'flakes' and combine with the lemon juice, soy, honey and crushed garlic.
- Add the chilli, scallions, lemongrass, shallots, coconut, almonds and prawns and coriander and toss well.
- Leave to stand for 1 hour for the flavours to develop, before serving.

Serves 2

Sweet and Sour Fish, 'Thai Style'

1 cup vegetable stock

1 onion, peeled and diced

200 g king fish, diced

1 cup sweet corn kernels

1 cucumber, seeded and sliced

1 cup pineapple,* diced

2 tomatoes, seeds removed

3 scallions

1 red bell pepper

2 tablespoons soy sauce

to taste salt and pepper

2 teaspoons cornflour, optional

- Place vegetables stock and onion in a saucepan and bring to the boil.
- Add the fish, sweet corn, cucumber, pineapple and tomatoes, and cover and simmer until just soft.
- Add scallions, bell pepper, soy and season to taste.
- Add more stock, if required, and simmer for a further 1-2 minutes. Thicken with cornflour blended with a little water, if desired.

Serves 2

*Note: If the pineapple is not a good ripe one, you may need to add up to 1 teaspoon of sugar (20 calories per teaspoon).

Steamed Custard in Pumpkin

1 small pumpkin (approx. 25 cm in diameter)

7 egg whites

250 ml low fat milk

75 ml apple concentrate (or 50 g palm sugar)

- Wash the pumpkin carefully. Cut the top off the pumpkin, by inserting a large sharp knife, in a circle about 5 cm from the stem. Save the top of the pumpkin as the lid. Remove the seeds.
- If necessary, trim a small slice from the base of the pumpkin to help it sit perfectly upright.
- Gently blend the egg whites, milk, apple concentrate, shredded coconut and salt. Pour into the pumpkin and place the lid back on.
- Steam for 30-60 minutes, depending on the thickness and type of pumpkin used.
- Serve hot or cold slice into wedges with a scoop of vanilla ice cream.

Serves 12

Gaang Hin Yaang
Grilled Rock Lobster Tail with Tamarind Dip

800 g rock lobster

For the Tamarind Dipping Sauce:
1 tablespoon tamarind juice
½ tablespoon nam pla
1 tablespoon shallots
25 g green lettuce leaves
handful coriander leaves
1 red chilli, sliced

- Slice the rock lobsters in half and remove the shells. Wash the lobsters and remove the intestinal tract.
- Grill over an open-fire until cooked, about- minutes.
- Serve with Tamarind dip garnished with coriander leaves, sliced red chillis and green lettuce.

To make the Tamarind Dipping Sauce
- Combine the tamarind juice with the shallots and nam pla in a small saucepan.
- Bring the mixture to a boil and stir until it thickens.

Serves 6-8

Yaam Polamai
Herbed Salad with Assorted Fresh Fruits

3 g salt
1 g sugar
1 teaspoon lime juice
20 g pomelo, cut in small dice
15 g tangerine, cut in small dice
8 g jicama yam beans
14 g red and green apple
50 g prawns, cooked, peeled and sliced
5 g roasted crispy garlic
5 g roasted crispy shallots
handful coriander leaves
1 red chilli, sliced

- Combine the salt, sugar and lime juice in a medium bowl.
- Toss through the diced fruits and prawns until well-coated.
- Sprinkle with the roasted crispy garlic and shallots, and garnish with coriander leaves and the sliced red chilli.

Serves 1

Tom Gai Prung
Chicken Soup with Ginger

2½ cups water

8 g lemongrass, sliced

8 g greater galangal

10 g ginger

20 g shallots

80 g chicken breast, sliced

2 tablespoons lime juice

2 tablespoons nam pla

3 g kaffir lime leaves, sliced

- In a medium saucepan, bring the water to a boil and add the sliced lemon grass, greater galangal, ginger and shallots.
- Leave it to simmer for a few minutes, and then add the sliced chicken breast, lime juice and shallots.
- Garnish with sliced kaffir lime leaves and serve immediately.

Serves 2

Yaam Thua Pu
Spicy Winged Bean Salad

½ tablespoon chilli jam

⅓ tablespoon salt

1 g sugar

1–1½ tablespoons lime juice

90 g winged beans, sliced

7 g shallots, sliced

800 g prawns, cooked and peeled

handful coriander leaves

1 red chilli, sliced

- Combine the chilli jam with the salt, sugar and lime juice to make the dressing.
- Blanch the winged beans in boiling water, then refresh in cold water, drain.
- Coat the beans, prawns and shallots in the dressing.
- Garnish with the coriander leaves and sliced red chilli.

Serves 6-8 persons

evason hua hin resort, thailand

Travel three hours by car from Bangkok to an *unspoiled paradise,* carefully created in *harmony* with the environment and cultural surroundings.

Essentially a fishing village in character, the seclusion of Pranburi exists only because it had *slumbered for years* in total obscurity.

The aim of Evason Hideaway resorts is to create innovative and enriching experiences in a *sustainable environment*. Suites provide *generous personal space* and offer *modern luxury* by appealing to all the senses: sight, sound, smell, taste, touch … and beyond. Attention to *detail and focus* on the reality of the destination is the driving force, together with a focused *commitment* to the environment. An extensive *organic* vegetable garden supplies the restaurants with produce, and seafood from the *local catch* features heavily on the menu.

The hotel supports the King's Cup Elephant Polo Tournament held every year in September to raise money for the well-being of elephants, who are under threat as their *traditional work* of logging becomes scarce. Several teams from Thailand, Australia and Sri lanka meet, using elongated polo sticks for two chukkas of 10 minutes per game. Proceeds go towards the running of the *elephant hospital*.

The Royal Project, initiated by the King of Thailand, is overseen locally by Prince Bhistej Rajani to motivate farmers to grow fruit and vegetables or produce handicrafts to substitute the poppies previously grown for the opium trade. Poppy crops have been virtually eradicated from the area since the inception of this project.

Slice a fresh aloe vera leaf straight down the centre; remove the clear, green gel and apply directly on to scalds, sunburn and itching or use as a soothing digestive tonic.

Sugar Cane Juice

The green liquid extracted from sugar cane stalks is a popular drink found in wet markets, roadside stalls and supermarkets throughout Asia. $1/2$ glass of freshly squeezed sugar cane juice mixed with 1 tablespoon of fresh ginger juice gives a thirst quenching drink which helps to remove toxins from the body. Included in the long list of health-giving benefits, the juice from this handy little perennial is attributed to relieving fever, vomiting, to ease mild oedema during pregnancy, and to facilitate or prevent measles.

Bircher Muesli

200 g rolled oats
600 g natural yogurt
120 g black raisins
60 g hazelnuts, peeled, crushed
400 ml fresh orange juice
80 g honey
2 green apples, julienned

- Combine all ingredients in a bowl, and leave overnight in refrigerator or for at least 30 minutes, so that the oats can soften.
- Gently fold apple through muesli and serve.

Serves 4

Egg White Omelette

12 egg whites
2 ripe tomatoes, diced
100 g scallions, finely sliced

- Whisk egg whites for 30 seconds until frothy.
- Place egg whites in a non-stick pan and cook over medium heat.
- When the omelette starts to brown at the edges, sprinkle tomato and onion over the top.
- Flip the two edges of the omelette in towards the centre so that an oval shape is formed.
- Cook with seam side down for a few seconds.
- Serve with Breakfast Tomatoes.

Serves 2

Breakfast Tomatoes

- Slice tomatoes in half and place on lightly greased baking tray or baking dish. Sprinkle over some olive oil, salt, freshly ground black pepper and a little sugar.
- Bake in a slow oven, 140°C until soft. Alternately, grill them under a broiler.

Asian Minestrone

5 ml vegetables oil
40 g celery, finely diced
80 g siew pak choy, washed and sliced
40 g snake beans, sliced ½ cm thick
50 g capsicum, finely diced
4 baby corn, sliced ½ cm thick
5 g lemongrass, about 10 cm
100 ml water
400 ml tomato juice
15 ml nam pla
10 ml light soy sauce
20 ml lime juice
2 kaffir lime leaves, finely sliced
5 g coriander, finely chopped

- Heat oil in saucepan and sweat the celery, siew pak choy, snake beans, capsicum, baby corn and lemongrass, quickly until colours become brighter.
- Pour in the water and tomato juice then stir in the nam pla, soy sauce, and lime juice, and bring to a boil.
- Lastly add the lime leaf and coriander and remove from heat.
- Garnish with a little extra coriander.

*Flavour of the soup improves if made one day in advance.

Serves 2

Thai Apple-Celery Salad

20 ml lemon juice
30 ml nam pla
sugar to taste
10 g red chilli
2 red apples
2 green apples
200 g celery sticks
20 g fresh mint leaf
4 green apples, hollowed out and brushed with extra lemon juice
4 red apples, hollowed out and brushed with extra lemon juice

- Combine lemon juice, nam pla, sugar and chilli in a bowl.
- Peel apples and remove strings from celery. Cut celery into 4 cm lengths, not too fine.
- Coat apple and celery with the dressing. Leave to marinate with sliced mint for 30 minutes.
- Spoon salad into prepared apples. Serve immediately.

Serves 4

Papaya Face or Body Mask

Papaya contains *papain*, an enzyme which helps to dissolve and remove

dry skin. Apply this mask once a week to give your skin a wonderful glow.

Blend the freshly mashed pulp of a ripe papaya with 2 tablespoons of fresh

pineapple juice. Leave on for 15 minutes then rinse off and moisturise as usual.

Caution: Can irritate highly sensitive or sunburned skin.

Pumpkin Soup

1 large leek, white part only, washed well
1 tablespoon olive oil
1 kg pumpkin, cut in 5 cm chunks, skin removed
5 cm piece ginger, peeled and finely chopped
2 stalks lemongrass, trimmed to 8 cm and thinly sliced
2 tablespoons ground cumin
1 litre vegetable or chicken stock
salt and black pepper to taste

- Slice the leeks across in 1 cm thickness.
- Heat oil in a large saucepan and sweat the leek until soft and transparent.
- Add ginger, lemongrass and cumin and cook for two minutes, until fragrant.
- Add pumpkin and cover with stock. Bring to a boil, then simmer until pumpkin is tender, about 20 minutes.
- Purée soup in an electric blender; strain, if necessary. Return soup to saucepan and season with salt and pepper.

Serves 4-6

To **soften leaf gelatine**, cover in cold water for 5 minutes or until very soft. Remove with your hand and squeeze out excess water. Add directly into a hot mixture, or melt in a bain-marie over low heat before adding to a cold mixture.

82

Vegetable Terrine

425 ml vegetable, chicken or veal stock
75 ml sherry vinegar
2 cloves garlic
2 sprigs thyme
1 teaspoon salt
black pepper to taste
8 leaves gelatin, softened in cold water
500 g mushrooms, sliced
1 tablespoon olive oil
500 g zucchini, thinly sliced lengthways

To make the terrine:
- Line a 1 litre terrine mold with plastic wrap.
- Sweat the mushrooms in olive oil until soft; drain excess liquid into a saucepan. Place the stock sherry vinegar, garlic, thyme, salt and pepper in a saucepan containing mushroom liquid and bring to the boil.
- Reduce heat and simmer over low heat for 10 minutes. Strain through a fine sieve or muslin cloth.
- Add softened gelatin to the strained liquid, stir well and leave aside until cool, and thick.
- Line the mold with zucchini strips, leaving a large overhang. Pour ½ cup of the jelly into the terrine to cover the base.
- Spoon about ⅓ of the mushrooms into the terrine, and cover with the sloppy jelly. Repeat until the terrine is full; cover the top with remaining zucchini slices. Fold the remaining plastic wrap over the top and refrigerate overnight.
- Remove the terrine from the mold by gently tugging the plastic wrap to loosen it. Place the mold onto a serving plate or cutting board and lift mold, then remove the plastic wrap.
- Slice and serve with some cherry tomato, garnished with steamed rice, fresh herbs and ground chilli.

Caesar Salad with Black Pepper Beef

300 g sirloin beef
salt to season
80 g crushed black pepper
2 heads romaine lettuce, medium size, washed
60 g semi-dried tomatoes
80 g grated parmesan
100 g croutons
250 ml Caesar Dressing

For the Caesar Dressing:
2 egg yolks
2 anchovy fillets, finely chopped
10 g garlic, peeled and chopped
20 ml white vinegar
salt and black pepper to taste
150 ml sunflower oil
20 g grated parmesan

- Heat oven to 220°C.
- Season beef with salt and cover with crushed black pepper.
- Roast meat in a hot oven for 22 minutes, or until medium rare. Leave aside to cool, then slice thinly.
- Carefully break lettuce leaves into 5 cm pieces.
- Toss lettuce with dressing, then place on 4 serving plates. Arrange slices of beef on lettuce, then semi-dried tomatoes and parmesan.
- Make the dressing by whisking egg yolks, chopped anchovies, garlic, white vinegar in a bowl. Add oil, one spoonful at a time, until dressing is thick, however it can be thinned down later with a little water, if preferred.
- Can be thinned down with a little water, if preferred.
- Stir in grated parmesan.

Serves 4

Grape Terrine

250 ml water
250 ml white wine
120 g sugar
35 g leaf gelatine
110 g green grapes, seeds removed
110 g red grapes, seeds removed

- Bring water, wine and sugar to a boil.
- Soak gelatine in a bowl of cold water for a few minutes to soften.
- Squeeze the water from the gelatine and add to the sugar-wine mixture, stirring well to ensure the gelatine dissolves properly. Leave to cool slightly.
- Line a terrine mould or desired shape jelly molds with the grapes, then pour over the jelly mixture.
- Refrigerate for at least 6 hours.
- To unmold the jelly, place the base of the mold into hot water for a few seconds, then invert onto a plate.
- Slice and serve with a berry coulis or sorbet.

Serves 6

Squid with Red Curry

50 g red curry paste
400 g squid tubes, cleaned
200 g snake beans
2 g sweet Thai basil
1 g long red chilli, cut lengthways in quarters
200 ml coconut milk
4 tablespoons nam pla
1 teaspoon white sugar
1 egg white omelette, made with 4 egg whites
200 g jasmine rice

- Cut open the squid tube to make a flat piece. With a sharp knife, score the flesh on the inner side making a diagonal pattern but without cutting the flexh through.
- Cut squid into strips about 8 x 5 cm.
- Sweat the curry paste in a non-stick pan, until fragrant. Add squid and toss over medium heat for 1 minute.
- Add long beans, basil and chilli and cook for 1 minute. Add coconut milk, nam pla and sugar and heat gently until almost boiling.
- Serve with fried egg white on top of steamed rice.

Serves 4

A Thai meal should achieve a harmonious balance of the four S's of flavour: spicy, sweet, sour and salty. Each item should offer contrasting textures, be visually appealing and exude its own subtle aroma. The interplay of herbs and spices to create these elements involves careful construction. Thai cuisine appears inextricably associated with chillies, but this popular misconception overlooks the vast number of dishes in Thai cuisine containing no chilli at all.

Thais believe that chillis detoxify the body, as well as ridding the body of flatulence, aiding digestion and relieving stomach cramps.

Some say Portuguese merchants brought the chilli back from Europe in the 16th Century; others believe it came across the Pacific on Spanish galleons via Mexico and Manila. Before its arrival, Thai cooks used black pepper, the locally grown prik thai, blended with strong aromatic spices and herbs, such as garlic, galangal and ginger. Of the dozen or so varieties of chilli used in Thai cuisine, three main types arise. The tiny red prik khi nuu, literally "mouse drop chilli" is the strongest and is usually served as an accompaniment, so that you have some control over the heat of the dish.

The long slender prik chi fah, "pointing skyward chilli", appears raw and cooked in many curries, as well as salads and stir-fries.

The tamest is the prik tuak "banana stalk chilli", generally roasted or par-boiled before being added to dishes.

four seasons resort at chiang mai, thailand

Escape Bangkok's *steaming*, thriving streets and make your way to the cool, clean and richly green hills of Thailand's north.

'Lanna' literally means land of a million rice fields. Four Seasons Resort at Chiang Mai is built in a gentle arc around *watery green rice paddies*, based on the architectural style of Thailand's ancient Lanna kingdom. The Lanna Spa is truly a *temple for the senses* where guests enjoy inner peace and outer pampering.

The resort's investment in and support of the local community is highlighted in the use of local cottons, silks and Sa paper products. Hand-woven, naturally dyed cottons are used for the soft furnishings and uniforms. A distinguishing decorative feature found throughout the resort is the inclusion of many carved wooden finials known as ngao, inspired by the gables of the roofs of the Lanna kingdom, and are now being crafted by local carpenters.

Incorporated into the landscaping picture is a *working rice farm* complete with its own family of *water buffalo*. The animals assist the rice farmers with preparation of the land for planting the rice and during the *harvest* process. The rice harvested is donated to local hill tribe villages through the assistance of the Royal Project, and over 10% of the produce used in the resort is supplied by *local Royal Projects*.

Day trips to the surrounding jungle include a float trip on *bamboo rafts*, an elephant safari, an authentic day-long trek to see *hill-tribe villages*, and exploring the city's famous *night bazaar*.

"Take only pictures and leave only footprints"

As calm as a Buddhist temple with a blissful peace and meditative silence.

For a traditional Thai hair restorative and conditioner, blend 2 tablespoons of fresh aloe gel with 1 kaffir lime to make a smooth paste. Apply to shampooed hair and leave on for 20 minutes, before rinsing off with cold water.

Lemongrass Sunrise

120 ml lemongrass tea
60 ml mango juice
60 ml pineapple juice
60 ml orange juice
1 tablespoon lime juice
1 tablespoon honey

- Shake all ingredients well, over ice.
- Serve in a tall glass spiked with sliced lime, a lemongrass stick and an orchid.

Narm Prig Noom
Green Chilli Paste served with Vegetables

10 green jalapeno peppers, grilled and skins removed
3 shallots, grilled
2 cloves garlic, grilled
1 eggplant, grilled and skin removed

- Place grilled peppers in a pestle and mortar and pound them a little.
- Add shallot, garlic and eggplant, and pound until smooth.
- Serve as a dip with boiled egg, crispy pork crackling, steamed vegetables such as cabbage, pumpkin, long beans, cauliflower, or other vegetables you may prefer.

Serves 2

Green Mango Salad

150 g green mango, shredded

20 g shallot, finely sliced

20 g dried shrimp

10 g chilli, sliced

20 g carrot, cut in julienne

20 g red and white cabbage, chiffonade

For the dressing:

40 ml nam pla

40 ml lime juice

20 g palm sugar

20 g sweet chilli paste

- Stir the dressing ingredients together in a small bowl.
- Combine ingredients in a bowl and coat well with the dressing.

Serves 2

Green mangoes are the firm, tart, under-ripe fruit, which are shredded for salads or cut into chunks before dipping in a sauce to be eaten as a snack. Don't be fooled by the colour of the skin, as a ripe mango can have a green skin.

Kaow Phod Poo
Corn Soup with Crab Meat

50 g fresh sweet corn kernels

2 medium ears

20 g crab meat

50 g onion, sliced

2 cups water

salt and white pepper to taste

cornflour to thicken

4 crab claws, for garnish

1 tablespoon chopped chives

- Place the water, sweet corn and onion in a pot. Bring to the boil and simmer until corn and onions are soft.
- Blend in a food processor and and strain through a sieve.
- Thicken with cornflour and water, if desired.
- Heat corn soup with crab meat; season with salt and pepper.
- Garnish with crab claws and chives.

Serves 2

Lemongrass Yam Noodle Salad with Shrimp

- 100 g yam noodle
- 20 g dried shrimp
- 20 g cashew nuts
- 20 g lemongrass, sliced
- 10 g kaffir lime leaves, chiffonade
- 20 g shallots, finely sliced
- 20 g mint leaves
- 3 large shrimp
- 40 ml Sweet and Spicy Chilli Sauce

- Combine all ingredients together in a bowl. Place on serving dish.

Serves 1

Sweet and Spicy Chilli Sauce

- 2 tablespoons lime juice
- 2 tablespoons fish sauce
- 1 tablespoon palm sugar
- 1½ tablespoons sweet chilli paste

- Mix all ingredients together and stir until dissolved.

Kaeng Pah Jay Spicy Jungle Curry

- 20 g red curry paste
- 1 litre vegetable stock
- 5 g kaffir lime leaves
- 20 g small eggplant
- 20 g long bean
- 20 g baby corn
- 20 g bamboo shoot
- 20 g pumpkin
- 20 g straw mushrooms, cut vertically in half
- 10 g rhizome
- 10 g green peppercorn
- 40 ml white mushroom soy sauce
- 10 g red green and yellow chilli
- 10 g Thai basil leaves

- Heat the wok and add the curry paste.
- Add vegetable stock and other vegetables except chillies and basil.
- Season with soy sauce, then stir in the chillies and basil leaves.

Serves 2

Thai Style Barbecue Chicken

1 whole chicken, cut in half
4 coriander roots, finely chopped
2 large garlic cloves, finely chopped
1 teaspoon white pepper
2 tablespoons oyster sauce
1 tablespoon dark soy sauce
1 tablespoon palm sugar
1 tablespoon vegetable oil
1 tablespoon mushroom soy sauce
2 tablespoons red Thai curry paste

- In a small bowl, combine coriander root, garlic, white pepper, oyster sauce, black soy sauce, palm sugar, vegetable oil, mushroom soy sauce and red curry paste.
- Coat the chicken in this mixture and marinate for at least 2 hours.
- Heat the grill, and cook the chicken until done, about 20 minutes. You will be able to tell the meat is cooked when the juices run clear after a skewer is inserted into the flesh.
- Serve with Spicy Sour Sauce (see below).

Serves 2

Spicy Sour Sauce

2.5 cm piece galangal, finely chopped
2 coriander roots, finely chopped
1 clove garlic, minced
2 tablespoons Tamarind Water (see recipe page 105)
sugar to taste
1 tablespoon chilli powder
2 tablespoons nam pla

- Combine all ingredients together in a bowl. Sugar to taste; the sauce should be sour, salty, spicy and sweet.

Poached Salmon with Lime

For the poaching liquid:
1 litre water
½ tablespoon nam pla
2 tablespoons lime juice
5 cm piece ginger, peeled and sliced
2 scallions, cut in 5 cm lengths
2 x 180 g salmon steaks
2 blanched cabbage leaves
pak pring chillies

1 lime, sliced in wedges
handful coriander leaves
1 red chilli, sliced

For the Spicy Sauce:
40 ml nam pla
40 ml lime juice
sugar, to taste
chopped chilli, to taste
chopped garlic, to taste

- Make the Spicy Sauce by stirring all ingredients in a small bowl together.
- Place the water, nam pla, lime juice, ginger and scallions in a pan and bring to the boil, then simmer for 3 minutes.
- Poach the salmon by sliding them into the barely simmering liquid. Turn the heat up a little but do not allow it to boil. Cook for 5 minutes, then turn off the heat and leave the salmon steaks in the liquid for another 1–2 minutes, depending on thickness. Drain salmon steaks on paper towel before serving on plate.
- Arrange cabbage and pak pring on serving plates and place fish on top.
- Spoon a little of the sauce over, then sprinkle with coriander leaves and chilli. Serve with lime wedges.

Serves 2

amanpuri, phuket, thailand

Amanpuri in Sanskrit, means "Place of Peace."

Sprawling across an *old coconut plantation*, its white-sand beaches, glacier-clear water and *vertiginous limestone cliffs* have, for many years, drawn visitors – not just for the scenery, but also for profitable adventure. Until half a century ago, the waters around Phuket were notorious hunting grounds for pirates who hid in the network of *secret coves* along the coast and in the *outlying islands*.

Today you can *potter around in boats*, go snorkelling among the *corals* and explore the *shimmering grottoes* and tiny tucked away beaches of the Andaman Sea. These are just some of the reasons that so many guests return to *Amanpuri*, and to facilitate these pleasurable activities, the owners took the *exacting standards* of Amanpuri on land and replicated them on water, thus creating Amancruises. Prior to the recent tsunami, Amanpuri's fleet of 20 boats, was considered, as a collection of boats used exclusively by guests staying at a property, to be the finest in the world. Amanresorts advise that they are well on the way to restoring that ranking.

Aman Spa advocates a *lifestyle approach* to wellness. Individualised assessment is followed by a *tailor-made programme* that focuses on holistic therapies as well as traditional beauty treatments.

The *Look Pra Kob* body treatment combines the use of a heated pumice filled with native Thai herbs, with a traditional Oriental oil massage. A Thai herbal steam concludes the treatment.

Ancient Thai Herbal Scrub combines clay, rice, turmeric, plai, galanga and magrut to *refresh the spirit* and tighten the skin.

Mesmerising views through coconut palms.
A sweet whiff of frangipani.
Dial N for Nirvana ...

Asian Pennywort

More fashionably known as 'gotu kola', this small, creeping herb is recognised throughout Asia for its many medicinal properties.

The cooling green juice which is rich in Vitamin A is said to be "good for the eyes", reduces fever, purifies the blood, cures nervous conditions, improves memory, relieves heartburn, headaches and burns . . .

Sometimes sold as 'arthritis herb' in western nurseries, it is said that eating 2 leaves per day will relieve arthritis.

Whilst readily available in cans from Asian fast food vendors, the juice has much more appeal when made from fresh leaves, sweetened with a little sugar syrup and poured over crushed ice.

The leaves have a slightly bitter tang and make a good salad combined with shallots and lightly seasoned with lime juice and chilli, topped with freshly grated coconut.

Nam Bai Bua Bok
Asian Pennywort Cocktail

500 g Asian pennywort, washed

30 ml water

1 teaspoon sugar syrup

crushed ice

- Place leaves in blender with water, sugar syrup and a little crushed ice.
- Blend until smooth and pour into a chilled glass and serve.

Mushroom Herb Omelette

90 g egg white (approx 3)
1 teaspoon grapeseed oil
3 tablespoons sliced mushrooms
pinch each of fresh and finely chopped thyme, basil and parsley

- Heat oil in a non-stick pan and sauté the mushrooms with a little salt and pepper. Sprinkle in herbs.
- Pour in the egg whites, stirring twice to avoid breaking them up too much.
- Slide the eggs to the front of the pan by tilting it gently. Flip the two edges of the eggs in towards the centre so that an oval shape is formed. Cook with seam side down for a few seconds.
- Remove and drain omelette on paper towel to absorb oil. Serve with slices of pineapple, tomato and some bean sprouts.

Soy Pancakes with Apricot Sauce

2 cups plain flour **1 cup yoghurt**
½ cup soy flour **1 tablespoon honey**
1 tablespoon bicarb soda **30 g egg white (approx 1)**
½ tablespoon salt

- Sift all dry ingredients together in a large bowl.
- Combine yoghurt and honey in a small bowl and add to the dry ingredients. Beat egg white until stiff and fold into the pancake mixture.
- Cook the pancakes in a hot and lightly greased non-stick pan.

Apricot Sauce

6 ripe apricots, halved with stones removed **1 vanilla bean, split**
½ cup sugar **2 tablespoons yoghurt**

- Place apricots in a small saucepan. Add just enough water to cover them. Add sugar and vanilla and gently bring to the boil. Simmer fruit over low heat until soft and mushy.
- Remove fruit with a slotted spoon and place in a blender. Reserve any remaining liquid.
- Blend until smooth, and leave to cool completely. Add yoghurt and adjust sweetness and consistency, if required, by adding a little of the cooking liquid.

Wholesome, flavoursome food that nourishes body and soul

Tom Yaam Pla Nam Sai
Spiced Fish Soup

1 litre light fish stock or water

2 tablespoons greater galangal cut in julienne strips

4 tablespoons sliced lemongrass

2 teaspoons chilli, sliced

2 shallots, sliced

4 kaffir lime leaves, chiffonade

200 g skinless fish, snapper, perch, mackerel, sliced

25 g straw or button mushrooms, quartered

2 tablespoons nam pla

4 tablespoons lime juice

2 teaspoons sugar

2 teaspoons fresh coriander

- Heat stock in a medium saucepan, add galangal, lemongrass, chilli, shallots, lime leaf, fish and mushrooms and heat until almost boiling.
- Season with nam pla, lime juice and sugar and season to taste with salt and pepper. Simmer until fish is just cooked, about 2 minutes.
- Pour into serving bowls and garnish with fresh coriander leaves.

Serves 2

Paw Pia Soot
Fresh Spring Rolls with a Sweet Chilli Sauce

24 paw pia wrappers or Chinese Pancakes

240 g jicama, peeled and julienned

30 ml white mushroom soy sauce

1 teaspoon sugar

30 ml vegetable oil

1 cup bean sprouts, cleaned, blanched and refreshed

24 soft lettuce leaves

1 omelette made from 2 lightly whisked eggs, cut in 1 cm strips

¼ cup crispy shallots

¼ cup crispy slivered peanuts

24 medium prawns steamed, peeled, deveined and halved

240 g chicken breast, poached and shredded

¾ cup Paw Pia Sauce

- Heat oil in wok until medium hot and sauté jicama. Stir in soy sauce and sugar then leave aside. Mixture should be wet.
- To roll paw pia, lay out about 6 wrappers at a time. Cover the bottom third with lettuce leaving a 3 cm border on each side. Place a strip of egg on top of lettuce and about one tablespoon each of jicama and bean sprouts.
- Place 2 prawn halves and about one tablespoon shredded chicken on top, then about ½ teaspoon each of shallots and peanuts. Drizzle ½ tablespoon of sauce over the lettuce and spread a little on the outer edge to seal the roll. Fold outside edges towards the centre, and roll from bottom to top, sealing with the sauce spread edge.
- Cut each roll in half on the bias and serve with additional sauce.

Makes 24

Paw Pia Sauce

100 g dried prik chee faa, chile "annum longum"

1 cup Tamarind Water

2 cups palm sugar

1 cup white mushroom soy sauce

½ teaspoon salt

- Remove seeds and tops from dried chillies. Soak in hot water for about 30 minutes. Rinse and drain chillies and place in blender. Blend to a paste, adding only enough tamarind water to blend. Add remaining ingredients and bring to a boil, then simmer about 5 minutes. Cool and store in refrigerator until required.

Makes 2 cups

Tamarind Water

3 tablespoons tamarind pulp

375 ml warm water

- Soak the tamarind paste in warm water for 20 minutes.
- Squeeze the pulp with your fingers and stir well.
- Strain the mixture and discard the solids.

Fresh Sashimi Tuna

600 g fresh tuna, sliced finely

2½ tablespoons sesame seeds

1½ tablespoons grilled coconut

2½ tablespoons green onion, finely chopped

1½ tablespoons red chilli, finely chopped

1 tablespoon lime juice

1½ tablespoons dashi

½ tablespoon ginger juice

pepper leaves

Cucumber Relish

- Line plate with tuna slices.
- Sprinkle other ingredients over top. Garnish with pepper leaves and serve with Cucumber Relish.

Serves 1

Cucumber Relish

300 g cucumber peeled and finely diced

1 tablespoon mint leaves, finely sliced

1 tablespoon coriander, finely chopped

45 ml freshly squeezed lemon juice

pinch each of salt and sugar

1 green chilli, seeded and sliced

- Combine all ingredients together in a small bowl. Serve immediately.

Yaam Makuea Yow Eggplant Salad

70 g steamed shrimp, peeled and cut in half

200 g Japanese eggplant

70 g skinless chicken breast, poached and shredded

1 shallot, thinly sliced

1 red chilli, seeded and thinly sliced

1½ tablespoons lime juice

1½ tablespoons nam pla

½ tablespoon sugar

- Grill the outside of the eggplant over a hot flame so that the outside is charred and the inside is soft but not mushy.
- Cut them into 5-8cm slices, then peel the slices by splitting the skin and pulling it off.
- Arrange slices in a single layer on a serving plate.
- Place shrimp and chicken on top, followed by shallots and chilli.
- Dissolve the sugar in the lime juice and nam pla. Taste and correct seasoning if necessary – it should be salty, sour and sweet.
- Pour the dressing over the salad and serve.

Grilled Chicken Breast with Pepperonata and Lentils

2 medium onions, peeled and sliced

1 large red bell pepper, seeded and thinly sliced

1 large yellow bell pepper, seeded and thinly sliced

a little olive oil

4 vine-ripened tomatoes, concassee

2 tablespoons basil, chopped

pinch each of thyme, salt, white pepper

500 ml chicken stock

250 ml dried green lentils

1 bay leaf

1 shallot, peeled

1 clove garlic, flattened

1 cup sun-dried tomatoes, chopped

2 breast fillets of organic chicken marinated with olive oil, garlic and lemon zest. Skin can be removed, if desired

- Heat a little oil in a non-stick pan and sweat the onions and peppers until soft.
- Add tomato and cook until thickened. Season with salt and pepper and stir in basil; keep warm until serving.
- Heat stock, lentils, bay leaf, shallot and garlic in a small saucepan until boiling. Simmer until lentils are tender but firm.
- Remove shallot, garlic and bay leaf and season with a dash of olive oil, and stir in the sun-dried tomatoes. Leave aside until required.
- Grill chicken breast until just done, about 2 minutes on each side. Slice chicken on an angle.
- Place 4 tablespoons of lentils on each plate, then lay the chicken breast across and top with some of the Pepperonata. Serve immediately.

Serves 2

Pla Kapong Nueng Se-Ew Steamed Snapper with Vegetables

1 x 600 g snapper, scaled and cleaned

3 tablespoons green onion, cut in julienne strips

½ teaspoon ginger, cut in julienne strips

1½ teaspoon celery, cut in julienne strips

2 teaspoons red chilli, cut in julienne strips

3 tablespoons fish stock

2 teaspoons white mushroom soy sauce

2 teaspoons soy sauce

¼ teaspoon ground white pepper

- Make a stock with 1 cup of water and the vegetable and ginger trimmings.
- Steam fish over simmering stock until done, about 15 minutes, and place fish on a serving plate. Strain and retain fish juices, about ¼ cup.
- Mix the julienned vegetables and spread over the fish.
- In a small saucepan, heat the fish stock, soy sauces, white pepper and reserved fish juices. Pour over the vegetables and serve with lime wedges and steamed rice.

Serves 2

evason phuket resort, thailand

The Evason Phuket Resort, located at Rawai Beach on the south eastern side of Phuket Island, embodies the Evason philosophy of *redefining experiences*, and, as such, presents a *refreshing reinterpretation* of a five star resort whilst easily meeting all the requirements.

Local Thai herbs, flowers and aromatics such as tamarind juice and galangal are *traditionally blended* to create the body masks and scrubs used within their spa. Thai massage, a precious wisdom which has been passed down for generations to relieve anatomical anxiety, is also featured here as a sophisticated healing practice that can subdue various ailments.

A *precious wisdom* that has been passed down for generations, Thai massage is not only an activity that relieves anatomical anxiety, but also a sophisticated *healing practice* that can subdue various ailments. Its *long history*, stretching back some 2,500 years, reflects the structure of faith and healthcare philosophy so unique to this part of the world. *Sen*, the fundamental concept that underlies the entirety of Thai massage, is a curious notion indeed. Some see it as a form of *metaphysical energy*, a network of invisible conduits that transport the flowing *life-force* to different corners of the body. Others approach sen with less abstraction, explaining that it is in fact the *wondrous lace work* of tendons, tissues and muscles that hold the body in one piece.

The idea is that if you can *fix the bad sen* – a consequence of stress, overwork or even the malfunction of an organ – you can fix the mechanics of your body by *untangling* any complications. It's almost a *buddhist implication*: solving your problems by solving your *inner*

Ancient massage, or, Nuat bo'rarn, is translated as meaning "to touch with the intention to heal".

Correctly done, a soothing effect will take place inside the body as the complex layers of veins, membranes and tissue unwind in a relaxing mode, freeing the strained segments and promising, hopefully, peace of mind.

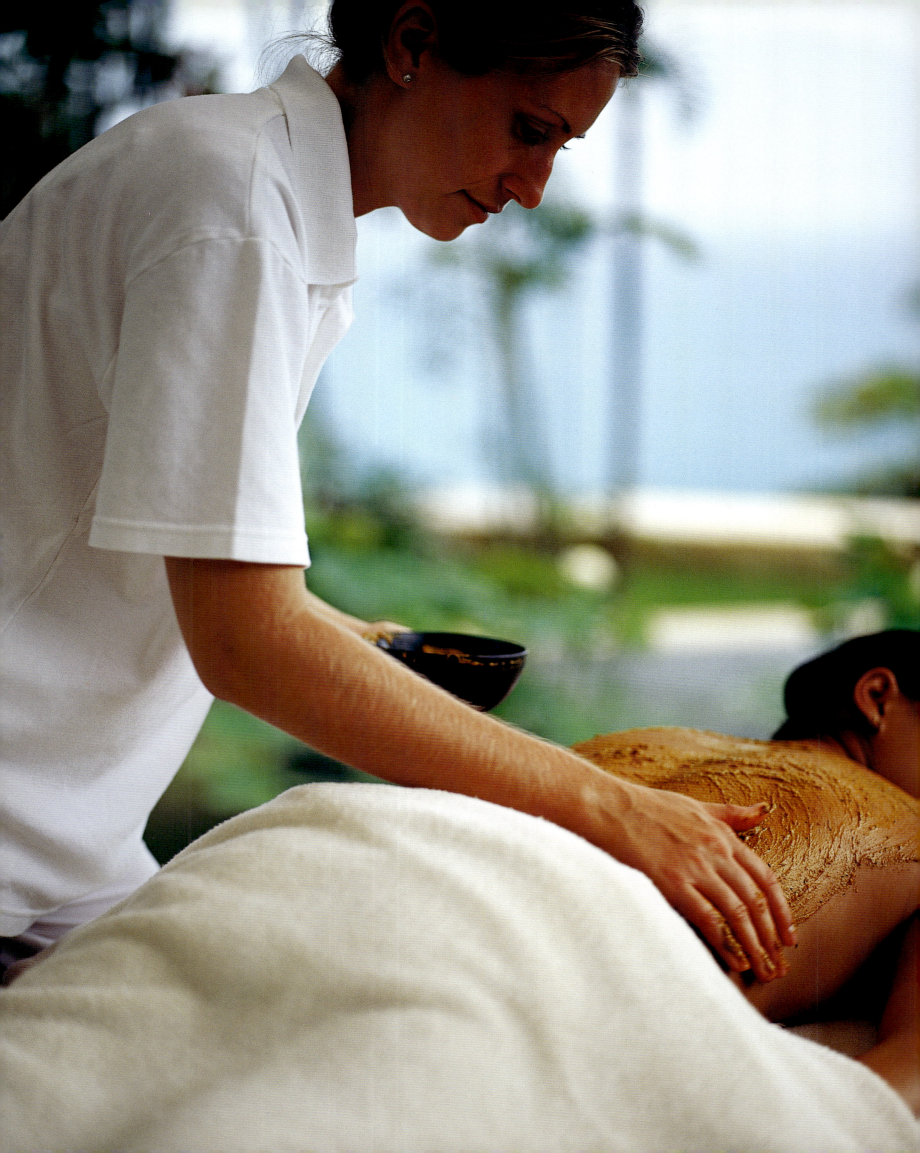

Miso Broth with Tatsoi-Enoki Salad

- 4 tablespoons yellow miso paste
- 2 thick slices ginger
- 1 litre dashi stock
- ½ tablespoon wasabi powder
- 1 tablespoon rice wine vinegar
- ½ tablespoon soy sauce
- 2 tablespoons scallions, green parts only cut into 3 mm slices
- ½ teaspoon sugar
- salt and black pepper, to taste
- 65 g enoki mushrooms
- 115 g tatsoi leaves or watercress
- 1 x 300 g cake of soft tofu, cut into four cubes

- Combine miso paste and ginger with the dashi stock and bring to a boil over a medium heat; simmer for 5 minutes and then remove the ginger.
- In a small bowl combine the wasabi powder and vinegar and stir to blend. Whisk in the soy sauce, scallions and sugar, then season with salt and pepper.
- Toss the enoki and tatsoi together; add the wasabi-flavoured vinegar and coat leaves well.
- Carefully place 1 slice of tofu into each of the four serving bowls. Ladle the broth over the tofu then carefully place a small mound of salad on each of the tofu portions and serve.

Serves 4

Carpaccio of Tuna with Ginger and Sesame Salad

- 4 x 70 g yellow fin tuna steaks, 2 cm thick
- 1 teaspoon groundnut oil
- ½ teaspoon castor sugar
- ½ teaspoon ginger, finely chopped
- ½ teaspoon red and green chilli, finely chopped
- 1 teaspoon sesame oil
- 1 teaspoon sesame seeds, lightly toasted
- sea salt
- 1 lime, halved
- 100 g mixed curly endive and sprouting beans (alfalfa, mung beans)

Dressing:
- Make the dressing in advance so it improves in flavour. Whisk together the groundnut oil, sugar, ginger, chillies and sesame oil, then stir in the sesame seeds and the salt.

The Tuna:
- Place each steak between two pieces of lightly-oiled cling film, and beat gently with a rolling pin until it is 2 mm thick.
Be very careful and keep turning the tuna as you beat it, so that you end up with a thin, round piece of tuna without holes. Leave in the cling-film and place
into the refrigerator until ready to serve.

To serve:
- Peel one side of the cling-film off the tuna and lay it face down onto a cold serving plate, then carefully remove the other half of the cling-film. Squeeze the lime juice over the tuna.
- Toss the salad leaves and sprouts in a little of the dressing and pile in the centre of the tuna. Sprinkle the remaining dressing over the tuna.

Mushroom Risotto

½ cup olive oil

6 shallots, finely chopped

2 cloves garlic, finely chopped

2 stalks lemongrass, white part only, finely sliced

1 tablespoon green peppercorns, flattened

125 g fresh shiitake mushrooms, thinly sliced

2 cups arborio rice

½ cup dry white wine

1 litre boiling vegetable or chicken stock

60 g cloud mushrooms, bases trimmed

To garnish:

8–12 crispy slices of pumpkin

bok choy sliced and lightly sautéed

2 tablespoons coriander pesto, moistened with extra olive oil

salt and pepper to taste

- Heat oil in a medium saucepan and when just hot, add shallots, garlic, lemongrass, and peppercorns and sweat them gently until shallots become transparent.
- Turn up heat to moderate and add shiitake mushrooms; cook for 1 minute. Add rice, and stir constantly for 2 minutes, then pour in wine and let it evaporate for 2 minutes.
- Add ½ cup of the stock to the rice and continue stirring with a wooden spoon for a few minutes. Keep adding ½ cup of stock at a time, only adding more stock when the liquid has been absorbed. Season to taste.
- When all the broth is incorporated the rice should be cooked but still with a "bite", usually about 16 minutes from when the first stock is added.
- Serve on warmed plates and top with sautéed bok choy and crispy pumpkin slices. Drizzle plates with Coriander Pesto.

Serves 4–6

Tuna Parfait with Two Caviars

225 ml double cream

225 g yellow fin tuna, cut into very small dice

3 dashes Tabasco

1 tablespoon chives, finely chopped

8 whole chives

1 tablespoon extra virgin olive oil

to taste salt and freshly ground black pepper

55 g wasabi Tobiko

55 g Osetra caviar

Vinaigrette:

½ tablespoon Dijon mustard

½ tablespoon rice wine vinegar

60 ml grape seed oil

1 tablespoon wasabi tobiko

salt and pepper to taste

- To make the vinaigrette, combine the mustard, vinegar and oil in a small bowl. Season with salt and pepper and whisk lightly. Gently stir in the tobiko.
- In a small chilled bowl, whip the cream until soft peaks form, and then set aside.
- Fill a large bowl with ice. Place a medium bowl in the ice and add the tuna, Tabasco sauce, chopped chives and olive oil. Season with salt and pepper to taste and mix lightly.
- Spray the insides of 4 x 2.5 cm ring moulds with non-stick cooking spray. Fill the molds with layers of mixture, as follows: ⅛ tuna mixture, ¼ tabiko, ⅛ tuna mixture, ¼ Osetra caviar.
- Press down lightly on the parfaits with each layer using the bottom of the Tabasco bottle. Top the parfaits with a thin layer of cream and smooth to cover. Unmold the parfaits onto 4 plates and garnish each portion with 2 chives.
- Drizzle the vinaigrette around the parfaits and serve with a small spoon.

Serves 4

Marinated Beef on Drunken Rice

500 g beef eye fillet, trimmed

2 handfuls watercress

Vanilla Balsamic Reduction (see recipe page 45)

For the marinade:
2 tablespoons dry sherry

2 tablespoons nam pla

½ cup mint leaves, roughly chopped

2 kaffir lime leaves, chiffonade

For the rice:
½ teaspoon salt

2 cloves garlic

2 large green chillies, seeds removed

1 stalk lemongrass

1 kaffir lime, zest only

2 shallots, peeled

1 cup arborio rice

2 tablespoons olive oil

500 ml vegetable or chicken stock

- Combine the marinade ingredients in a flat dish and leave the meat to marinate in it for at least one hour, preferably overnight.
- In a mortar and pestle or food processor, grind together the salt, garlic, chillies, lemon grass, lime zest and shallots to make a smooth paste. This can be made a few days ahead and kept refrigerated.
- Heat oil in a medium saucepan and add paste, cooking over medium heat until fragrant. Add rice and cook over heat for 1 minute, stirring constantly. Pour in stock and return to heat until boiling. Lower heat to a simmer, and cook until rice is soft, about 15 minutes, stirring occasionally.
- While the rice is cooking, heat the hotplate to grill beef on. Drain beef fillet and sprinkle or spray with a little olive oil. When plate is very hot, sear all sides of the meat for a 3-4 minutes. Leave beef aside to rest covered under a kitchen towel for 8 minutes before slicing.

To serve
- Spoon rice onto serving plates. Arrange slices of beef over rice and top with handful of watercress. Drizzle Vanilla Balsamic Reduction around plate.

Serves 2

Sesame Sweet Potato

4 large sweet potatoes, cut into chunks

15 ml vegetable oil

15 ml sesame oil

sea salt

- Brush the peeled long sweet potato slices with combined vegetable and sesame oil
- Sprinkle with sea salt and place in a 200ºC and bake until the sweet potato is golden.
- Serve as a hot vegetable side or cool and serve with salad greens and simple dressing.

Serves 4

Sesame Spinach

3 tablespoons white sesame seeds, toasted

½ teaspoon sugar

2 tablespoons light soy

3 tablespoons dashi

large pinch salt

500 g fresh spinach, well washed and drained

1 teaspoon vegetable oil

- Grind 2 tablespoons of the sesame seeds in a mortar and pestle, until smooth. Combine with the sugar, soy sauce and dashi to make the dressing. Leave aside.
- Heat oil in a non-stick pan and add the spinach leaves, a handful at a time. Stir with a wooden spoon, adding more leaves when those in the pan have wilted.
- Drain spinach in a colander, squeezing out excess moisture. Stir the dressing through the spinach and place in serving bowl. Serve either hot or at room temperature, topped with extra sesame seeds.

Serves 4

Oven-Roasted Cod Fillet with Curry Leaf Coconut Sauce

The Oven Roasted Cod Fillet:

600 g cod fillet, skinned

10 ml lemon juice

2 pinches salt

5 g ground fennel

5 g ground cloves

5 g ground chillies

The Curry Leaf Coconut Sauce:

70 ml vegetable oil

4 g mustard seeds

15 g ginger, chopped

15 g garlic, chopped

75 g onions, finely chopped

10 curry leaves

75 g tomatoes, chopped

3 g turmeric

4 g ground chillies

20 g cornflour

1 g ground cloves

2 g ground fennel

1 g red chillies

200 ml fresh coconut milk

The Dill Potatoes:

320 g new potatoes, cut into quarters

8 g ginger, chopped

8 g green chillies, chopped

2 g ground turmeric

20 ml olive oil

20 g dill

8 ml lemon juice

5 pinches salt

The Marinated Tomatoes:

250 g cherry tomatoes

10 ml olive oil

5 ml lemon juice

5 g brown sugar crystals

5 g black pepper, freshly ground

5 pinches salt

The Garnishes:

20 g carrot

20 g beetroot

20 g dill

20 ml Mint Oil (see glossary for Chive Oil and substitute chives for mint leaves)

pepper and lime to garnish

Oven-Roasted Cod Fillet:

- Heat oven to 200°C.
- Cut the cod fillet into 150 g portions. Place in a dish with the salt and lemon juice; marinate for 25 minutes.
- Combine the fennel, clove and chilli.
- Remove the cod from the marinade and pat dry on paper towels. Coat one side with the spice mixture.
- Heat some oil in a sauté pan over medium heat; sear the side of fish with the spice coating for 10–15 seconds and turn over. Place on a baking tray and bake in the pre-heated oven for 10 minutes. Keep warm until serving.
  Remove and keep warm.

Curry Leaf Coconut Sauce:

- Heat oil in a saucepan with mustard seeds over medium heat, until the seeds crackle. Add the chopped garlic, ginger and onions; sauté until fragrant and golden brown. Add half of the curry leaves, turmeric, chilli powder and chopped tomato and season with salt. Finally, add tamarind paste and stir well.
- Mix the corn flour with clove and fennel powder in a mixing bowl; add a little water to form a thick mixture. Remove and strain with a sieve. Add the remaining curry leaves and chilli and cook until fragrant. Pour in the coconut milk and adjust seasoning. Simmer for a few minutes; remove from heat and keep warm.

Dill Potato:

- Toss potatoes in olive oil in a baking dish and bake them for 20 minutes at 200°C. During the last 5 minutes of cooking, toss through the chopped ginger, garlic, salt, lemon juice and turmeric.
- Remove from oven; toss through the chopped dill and keep warm.

Marinated Tomato:

- Place the tomatoes in a mixing bowl; add olive oil and lemon juice. Stir well and season with sugar, pepper and salt. Refrigerate.

To serve

- Arrange some dill potatoes in the centre of serving plates, and place the oven-roasted cod on top. Spoon the marinated tomato on to the plate and drizzle with the Curry Leaf Coconut Sauce and Mint Oil. Garnish with crispy dill and vegetables. Serve immediately.

Serves 4

Iced Pineapple and Aniseed Mousse

120 g sugar

10 star anise

1 small pineapple, peeled and cut into small dice

zest of 2 lemons

50 ml fromage frais

50 ml Greek yoghurt

1 baby pineapple, cored

1 tablespoon honey

2 egg whites

1 tablespoon pink peppercorns, crushed

1 orange, zest and juice

90 g strawberries, thinly sliced

- In a heavy based saucepan, heat 100 g of the sugar with 1 tablespoon of water, star anise and pineapple over medium heat. Stir occasionally until the pineapple is soft. Liquidize in a food processor until smooth, and then pass through a fine sieve into a large bowl.

- Stir in the lemon zest, fromage frais and yoghurt. Place mixture into an ice cream machine and churn until nearly set.

- Heat the oven to 200ºC / gas mark 6.

- Cut the baby pineapple into 8 slices, four slices about 5 mm thick and four slices very thin. Peel the thicker slices and place onto a baking tray and bake for 15 minutes. Put the roasted pineapple into the base of 4 rings. Brush the very thin slices with honey on both sides. Place on a baking sheet and dry out in a very cool oven at 100ºC/gas mark ¼ for 3 hours until crisp.

- When the pineapple–yoghurt mixture is nearly frozen, bring the remaining sugar to the boil with 1 teaspoon of water over a high heat and boil until lightly caramelized.

- Whisk the egg whites until soft peaks form, then whisk in the caramel. Fold the egg white into the pineapple mixture and then pour it into the rings. Level the tops and place in the freezer for 2 hours.

- Place peppercorns, 1 teaspoon of sugar, orange zest and orange juice in a saucepan and heat for 3–4 minutes. Stir in strawberries, then remove from heat.

To serve:
- Slide a sharp hot knife around the insides of the rings and place the mousse onto cold serving plates.

- Place the crisp pineapple on top and decorate with the peppered strawberries.

Serves 4

marriott resort and spa
bangkok, thailand

Bangkok is stressful and confusing – no question about it.

A vast, flat gridlock, with streets and traffic confronting you from all *directions*. To my knowledge there are *no traffic rules*.

The *old quarter* clusters along the eastern bank of the Chao Phraya River, which meanders between Bangkok and Thonburi, the old capital. *Famous* for *R&R weekends* for American servicemen during the Vietnam War, then with a population of *1.5 million*, it rapidly grew to more than *10 million*. Now the *City of Angels*, as the Thais call it, represents to most of us, an urban nightmare. But amidst all the chaos, one soon comes to appreciate the *gentle nature* of the Thais and their *genuine respect* for other people.

A welcome glass of iced, *lemon grass tea* and a chilled flannel, handed to you upon entering the spa at The Bangkok Marriott Resort and Spa, will *restore your faith*. Try their *Thai Herbal Back Treatment*, the ultimate *subliminal body workout*. An exfoliating scrub of ground coriander bean, nutmeg and other spices *cleanse and revitalize* the skin, followed by a deep tissue massage, and ending with a warm compress of Thai herbs which is applied to the back to give added relief to *stressed muscles*.

Miang Kam Bai Chaa Plu: ginger, peanuts, roasted coconut meat, dried shrimp, chilli, shallot and lime, are all wrapped in these Cha Plu leaves to make the popular street food snack, which are then dipped in a sticky sweet tamarind sauce.

More than just air fresheners, *malai*, the garlands of jasmine hanging in the taxis, are seen as a protection against accidents. The ring of flowers is said to represent the buddha's teaching; its lifespan mirroring that of our own.

The life history of an individual can be told in one's hands; the nails keep no secrets.

Cleopatra was a devotee of soothing milk baths laced with yak's milk, essential oils and heady rose petals. This one, as indulgent as its namesake, suggests, will pamper the body and spirit and leave you with soft silky skin.

Cleopatra Bath

125 g powdered whole milk
1 tablespoon apricot kernel oil
10 ml jasmine oil
1 litre fragrant flower petals (optional)

- Pour milk powder and apricot kernel oil into the stream of a running bath.
- Add jasmine oil and scatter petals across the surface immediately before stepping into the tub.

Baked Chicken Breast with Lemongrass Sauce

200 g broccoli, steamed and finely chopped
50 g chopped onion
50 g boiled black beans
5 g each salt and pepper
2 chicken breast fillets, skin removed
30 ml olive oil
100 g arborio rice
100 g lemongrass
500 g chicken stock
10 g cornflower

- For the stuffing: Combine the broccoli, onion, black beans, salt and pepper.
- Heat oven to 180C.
- Insert a sharp knife along the side of each chicken fillet to create a pocket, then fill with the stuffing.
- Bake chicken breast between 15 to 20 minutes.
- In a small saucepan, heat olive oil and stir in arborio rice and lemongrass, stirring for 1 minute. Add chicken stock and bring to a boil, then simmer for 15 minutes.
- Puree in a blender until smooth. Strain.
- Reheat sauce and add 10 ml cornflour, season and stir until thickened.

Serves 2

Sautéed Chicken Livers

20 g garlic chopped
20 g shallots, sliced
1 teaspoon olive oil
15 g chicken liver, cleaned and trimmed
70 ml Demi-glace
2 tablespoons red wine
70 g grilled tomato
70 g green beans

- Sauté garlic and shallots in olive oil until soft. Add chicken liver, stirring until cooked through.
- Add demi glace and red wine to the pan and stir for one minute.
- Cook beans in boiling water until just tender.
- Spoon livers onto plate and garnish with grilled tomato and drained beans.

Serves 1

Demi-glace

250 ml brown veal or beef stock
2 teaspoons arrowroot
4 tablespoons Madeira
1 tablespoon tomato puree
2 tablespoons chopped mushrooms

- Dissolve arrowroot in Madeira and add to saucepan containing other ingredients. Bring to a boil and simmer until reduced to 250 ml. Strain; if desired, thicken sauce by whisking in 15 g unsalted butter.

Spicy Mushroom Salad

200 g straw mushrooms
50 g shallots
30 g scallions
2 tablespoons olive oil
salt and pepper to taste
20 ml red wine vinegar
30 g sweet basil leaves, sliced
10 g Chinkiang vinegar

- Blanch mushrooms in boiling water. Strain and refresh in ice water. Drain.
- Combine mushrooms with the remaining of the ingredients.
- Serve according to image.

Serves 1

Straw Mushrooms: Also known as paddy straw mushrooms after their most common growing environment — they grow on just about anything including dried water hyacinth leaves, dried legume leaves and chopped dried banana leaves.

Used in noodle dishes, soups and hotpots, these blackish–grey caps, seldom larger than a thumb with a very small stem are extremely high in protein. This places them as Asia's most important variety of fresh mushrooms. Once open they tend to be tough, so look for the more tender immature specimens.

Known as **nameko** in Japan and **hed fang** in Thailand, they have for a long time only been available outside of Asia in their dried form or in cans, although now are being commercially grown in Australia, US and Europe.

Spicy Wing Bean Salad

250 g sliced wing beans
2 boiled eggs, peeled and quartered
100 g minced chicken breast
50 g toasted cashew nut
30 g toasted, shredded coconut
10 g chilli, sliced
1 tablespoon sugar
1½ tablespoons lemon juice

- Lightly brush a non-stick frying pan with vegetable oil. Add chicken mince and cook over medium heat for a few minutes, until meat is cooked through. Leave aside to cool.
- Drain and then toss through the remaining ingredients.
- Arrange on plate and serve immediately.

Serves 1

Kaow Kluk Kapi

1 egg, beaten
50 g fried dried shrimp
20 g shrimp paste
25 ml vegetable oil
200 g steamed rice
30 g shallots, sliced
30 g mango flesh, cut in julienne strips
1 fried egg, sliced
50 g cucumber, sliced
50 g long beans, sliced thinly
30 g coriander sprigs
10 g dried chilli, deep fried

- Lightly oil a non-stick pan with vegetable oil. Heat over medium heat and pour in egg to make an omelette. Allow omelette to cool before cutting into thin strips.
- Place rice in a small mound on serving plate with remaining ingredients placed in separate piles, as condiments.

Serves 1

Sushi Kaow Soy

15 g instant dashi

45 ml boiling water

100 g steamed rice

50 g green mango, cut in julienne

30 g shredded coconut

15 g instant dashi

45 ml boiling water

15 ml soy sauce

30 g shallots, finely sliced

30 g sugar

200 g Cha Plu leaves

- Dissolve instant dashi in boiling water.
- Combine rice, dashi mixture, mango, coconut, soy sauce, shallots and sugar together.
- Spoon mixture onto cha plu leaves and roll them up lengthways.
- Cut crossways into slices, like sushi, and serve.

Serves 1

Clear Vegetable Soup

1 kg chicken bones

1 litre water

100 g onion

100 g celery

100 g carrot

1 tablespoon olive oil

50 g carrot, diced

50 g potato, diced

50 g pumpkin, diced

50 g grilled leeks, chopped

50 g celery, diced

50 g cabbage, chopped

salt and pepper to taste

- Place chicken bones, water, onions, celery and 100 g carrot in a stock pot, bring to a boil, and simmer for one hour.
- In a large saucepan heat oil and sweat diced carrot, potatoes and pumpkin for 1 minute over medium heat. Add leek, celery and cabbage.
- Strain the chicken stock into pot containing vegetables and simmer for 10 minutes. Season with salt and black pepper.

Serves 4

Gang Lieng Goong

30 g shrimp paste

50 g shallots

30 g greater galangal

5 g black peppercorns

15 g coriander root

50 g sweet basil leaves

100 g red snapper fillet, poached

20 g pepper

400 ml chicken stock

200 ml assorted Thai vegetables (white lettuce, luffa, straw mushroom, ivy leaf, pumpkin, baby corn

100 g shrimp, peeled and de-veined

- In a mortar and pestle, blend together shrimp paste, shallots, galangal, herbs, pepper and fish, and add to boiling chicken stock.
- Add the vegetables and shrimp and continue to boil for 3 minutes.
- Pour soup into serving bowl and serve immediately.

Serves 1

Chicken Tea Soup with Shark Fin

500 g minced chicken

100 g carrot, diced

100 g onion, diced

100 g garlic chives, chopped

100 g celery, diced

60 g greater galangal, chopped

10 g black pepper, crushed

30 g coriander, chopped

2 litres chicken stock

3 eggs

20 g shark fin, steamed and finely sliced

salt and pepper to taste

- Combine all ingredients, except shark fin, together in a saucepan, and simmer slowly, for about an hour, until thickened.
- Strain; season with salt and pepper and reheat.
- Serve in two or three cups and garnish with shark fin.

Serves 2-3

the datai, langkawi, malaysia

We have arrived in the jungle at night!

An absurdly lush tropical rain forest setting with *soothing energy* emanating from the trees. The air is dewy, dripping jungle air, spiked with jasmine, the humic tang of rain forest soil and with a strong hint of the sea. The pervasive calm is broken only by the crash of a wave.

The *tile-roofed pavilions* of The Datai, framed with bougainvillaea and frangipani, emerge slowly from the hillside like some *ancient stone temple*. Out of the darkness, candlelit villas appear scattered throughout the *sloping rain forest.*

Following the distant pings of a gamelan along a torch-lit jungle path to the villa, it is difficult not to be a bit distracted by the noises of the jungle creatures. But sleep is not difficult.

In the light of day, one realises that the forest is situated on a secluded white sand beach at the end of the Andaman Sea.

Activities to help uncover the *secrets of the forest* are planned by the *resident naturalist*, Irshad. Cruise in a traditional style boat along the Kilim river delta through the mangrove swamp to a fish farm. Four million year old rock formations rise out of the sea, past a wilderness studded with *mystical lakes* and bat caves.

A local guide will take you on a really tough walk, read *jungle trek*, into the primary rain forest around Teluk Datai. You'll need strong hiking boots, long pants and sleeves and mosquito repellant for the four-hour hike through virgin forest over streams, mangrove areas and climbing through the undergrowth.

More than just quiet, this resort is a totally laid-back nature retreat, where popular sports include bird watching, nature walks, kite flying, top-spinning and golf.

Treatments are given in an open pavillion above a forest stream, with the obligatory audience of giggling monkeys.

Orange, Mango and Pineapple Smoothie

250 g mango
200 g pineapple
200 ml orange juice
30 g ice
5 g honey

- Peel mango and pineapple and blend with orange juice, ice and honey.
- Strain and pour into a chilled serving glass.

Datai Punch

35 ml pineapple juice
35 ml orange juice
35 ml watermelon juice
35 ml honeydew melon juice
15 ml Grenadine
1 sprig mint leaves

- Blend all ingredients together in a cocktail shaker, over ice.

Avocado Salsa (see page 143)

1 avocado
juice of lime
1 teaspoon nam pla
handful coriander leaves, finely chopped

- Mash all ingredients together in a small bowl until smooth.

Gazpacho Andalusia

2 slices white bread
100 ml tomato juice
80 ml ketchup
2 teaspoons paprika
100 ml chilli sauce
15 ml extra virgin olive oil
150 g cucumber, peeled and diced
100 g red onion, sliced
100 g each yellow, red and green bell pepper, finely diced

500 g tomato cut in wedges
100 g celery, finely diced
30 g toasted almond flakes
3 boiled eggs, peeled and sliced
1 litre vegetable stock, chilled
few drops Tabasco
salt to taste
black pepper to taste
small bunch chives, finely chopped

- To make croutons, cut the bread into small cubes and place them on a baking sheet. Drizzle a little olive oil over them and bake in a low oven for about 20 minutes, until dry and crisp.
- In a large bowl combine tomato juice, ketchup, paprika, chilli sauce and olive oil.
- Keep aside a little of the finely diced cucumber, red onion and bell pepper for garnish.
- Add the remaining tomato, onion, bell peppers, cucumber, celery, almond flakes and boiled eggs to the tomato juice mixture and leave to marinate in refrigerator for 30 minutes.
- Blend with vegetable stock until smooth. Season with tabasco and salt and pepper to taste. Chill until serving. Garnish with chives.
- Pour into serving bowls and garnish with diced vegetable, chopped chives and croutons.

Serves 4

Lentil Salad with Avocado Salsa

75 g green lentils	100 g red bell pepper
75 g red lentils	30 ml red wine vinegar
75 g green lentils	80 ml corn oil
75 g yellow lentils	salt
100 g carrot	black pepper
60 g celery	15 g chives, finely chopped

- In one bowl place half of the green lentils with the red lentils, and in another bowl place the remaining green lentils with the yellow lentils. Cover both with cold water, and leave to soak for 3 hours, or overnight in the refrigerator.
- Drain the lentils, and in separate saucepans bring each to the boil. Lower heat and cook until tender, about 25 minutes. Turn heat off and leave for a further 5 minutes. Drain and leave to cool while preparing the other vegetables.
- Finely dice the carrot, celery and bell pepper. Blanch separately in boiling water, then refresh in cold water. Drain.
- Make the vinaigrette by combining the red wine vinegar, corn oil, salt, black pepper and chives in a small bowl.
- Combine the celery and carrot with the red and green lentils and pour half of the vinaigrette over. Coat well and leave to marinate for 10 minutes. Add bell pepper to yellow and green lentils, coat with vinaigrette and leave to marinate for 10 minutes.
- Place a mound of lentils, about 10 cm in diametre, in centre of a serving plate and top with a handful of mesclun salad leaves.
- Arrange the second lentil salad around the edge of the plate. Spoon some of the Avocado Salsa (recipe page 142) on the plate between the two salads. Squeeze a little lemon or lime juice over.

Serves 4

Gado-Gado

150 g carrot, cut in 6cm batons	**Dressing:**
150 g cucumber, cut in 6cm batons	100 g shallot, minced
	50 g garlic
100 g chinese swede, cut in 6cm batons	30 g ginger
	40 g lemongrass
100 g bean sprouts, tails removed	10 g candlenuts
	3 cm pandan leaf
200 g water spinach	500 ml coconut milk
100 g long beans	200 g brown sugar
3 boiled eggs	30 g small red chillies
2 cakes bean curd	1 tablespoon tamarind juice
	1 teaspoon salt
	1 teaspoon sugar

- Blanch the carrot, chinese swede, beansprouts (optional), water spinach and long beans separately, refreshing vegetables in ice cold water after removing them from the boiling water.
- Heat 1 tablespoon oil in a non-stick pan, and fry the bean curd cakes until golden brown. Drain on absorbent paper. When cool, slice thinly.

For the Dressing:
- Blend together the shallot, garlic, ginger, lemongrass, candlenuts and pandan until a smooth aromatic paste.
- Heat 1 tablespoon oil in a saucepan over medium heat and sweat the aromatics until fragrant. Add remaining ingredients and bring to the boil. Remove from heat and use as required. makes about 3 cups of dressing.
- Make bundles of carrot, cucumber and chinese swede and tie them together with the water spinach. Place in centre of serving plate, and arrange a fan of bean curd slices and other vegetables around the bundle. Serve with a small bowl of Gado-gado dressing and garnish with strips of spring onion or pandan.

Serves 4

Tomato Tartare with Green Beans

180 g green beans
120 g tomato, finely diced
20 g shallot, very finely chopped
5 g chives, finely chopped
5 ml Balsamic vinegar
180 ml whipping cream
5 ml red wine vinegar
salt to taste
black pepper, to taste
Chive Oil (optional)
200 g yellow frisee lettuce

- Blanch the green beans in boiling salted water for 2 minutes. Drain and refresh in ice cold water. Drain until required.
- For the tartare, combine the tomato, shallot, chives and balsamic vinegar in a small bowl. Chill until required. Whisk the cream until slightly thickened. Gently fold in the red wine vinegar, salt and pepper.
- Place a 8-10 cm ring mold on a serving plate. Squeeze a circle of chive oil around the inside of the ring. Place about 4 teaspoons of the tomato tartare in the centre and use the back of of the spoon to gently press it into the mold. Gently lift the ring and repeat procedure on other plates.
- Toss the beans with just enough cream mixture to coat and stack about ¼ cup of the beans on top of the tartare, leaving about 2 cm in from the edge of the tomato perimeter.
- Toss the frisse in a little olive oil and salt. Twist about 1/4 cup of the leaves in the palm of your hand to make a compact bundle and place the bundle on top of the beans.

Serves 4

Pumpkin Risotto

30 ml extra virgin olive oil
50 g shallot, finely chopped
5 g garlic, finely chopped
200 g arborio rice
3 g black pepper
2 g thyme sprigs
240 ml dry white wine
240 g yellow pumpkin, peeled, seeded and diced
2 litres chicken stock, simmering

- Heat oil in a medium saucepan. Add shallot and garlic and sweat until soft and translucent.
- Add the rice and stir until well coated and just starts to cook. Season with salt and pepper and add thyme and pumpkin and stir well.
- Add wine over high heat, and stir well. Reduce heat to medium and add ½ cup of chicken stock. Continue to stir as the rice cooks, adding another ½ cup of rice only when the liquid in the rice has been absorbed.
- Continue to cook this way, stirring the rice and adding stock, until all liquid is used. Remove thyme stems, as leaves will have already fallen off into the rice.
- Pile rice in a serving bowl and garnish with Tempura Vegetables, optional.

Serves 4

For the Vegetable Tempura

- Very gently stir 100 g flour, 160 ml iced water and 1 egg yolk together until smooth. Dip 3–4 stems of asparagus or batons of zucchini in the batter and deep-fry until pale, but crisp.

Cameron Highlands Strawberries with Basil Oil

12 strawberries
handful of purslane
8 ml basil oil
flowers for garnish
12 g sugar
1 g black pepper
6 ml Vanilla Balsamic Reduction
2 small leaves and 2 tops, opal basil

- Place the washed, hulled strawberries in a mixing bowl, add sugar, herbs, basil oil and salad and toss together.
- Toss the handful of purslane with a little bit of sugar and some basil oil.
- Arrange the herbs and salad on a plate. Sprinkle with pepper and drizzle some basil oil over the top. Dot some of the Vanilla Balsamic Reduction onto the plate and garnish with a few flowers.

Serves 1

Strawberry Salad with Passionfruit Sorbet

2 stalks lemongrass
500 ml water
250 g sugar
1 litre passion fruit puree
8 strawberries, quartered
1 passionfruit, pulp

Sorbet mixture:
- Smash lemongrass in a mortar and pestle and add to a saucepan containing the sugar and water.
- Bring to a rolling boil and remove from heat and cool completely.
- When cold stir in passionfruit puree and chill in the refrigerator.
- Churn sorbet mixture until slushy. Spoon into container and freeze until required.
- Place strawberries in a serving bowl. Top with two scoops of passionfruit sorbet.
- Drizzle passionfruit pulp over the top and decorate with pandan leaf.

Serves 4

the legian, bali

Feasting on black sticky rice, yogurt, fresh mango chunks and pandan syrup to the *sounds of the rolling surf...*

This is breakfast *heaven*.

The Legian, Bali is a place that understands *how to soothe*.

A strong sense of *harmony and tranquility* connects the contemporary architecture and the Balinese landscape, overlooking the garden, beach and Indian Ocean. The main pool falls seamlessly into a smaller pool below which seems to *meld into the ocean*.

Minimalist in their modern simplicity, the treatment rooms have timber themes and their *abundant airiness* allows a constant awareness of the ocean's proximity.

Wander over to The Club at the Legian, a nearby cluster of 11 villas, each with their own dining bale overlooking a 10 metre pool. An even more personalised form of mind and body renewal is provided here, where guests can enjoy spa treatments and meals (with the assistance of their own butler), without ever having to leave their private *sanctuary* for the entire duration of their stay. Emerge from your *personal haven*, if you need to, for a spa meal or drink in the private lounge overlooking the Club's 35 metre pool.

Gamelan music pervades the sun-dappled stone walkways, bordered by lily ponds which link the 67 impressive suites.

The Chinese told time by it.

Japanese geishas used it to compute the cost of their client's entertainment.

Apart from driving away mosquitoes and creating a pleasant aroma, incense is used by the Thais as a cure for the common cold.

Originally made from **frankincense and myrrh** – other ingredients used are sandalwood, ambergris, basil, benzoin, camphor, clove jasmine, musk and patchouli.

It's subtle, pervasive fragrance fills countless temples, evoking the **spirit of the Orient**. The heady scent and lazy curls of smoke speak of a different place, a different time.

Incense presented with food is not part of the gift; the smoke serves merely as a **signal to the spirits** that a meal has been prepared for them. Smoke rising upward symbolises prayer, making the offering synonymous with worship. Lighting the incense engages the spirits in conversation, the smoke serving as **a link between man and divine powers**. When the stick is consumed, contact with the other world is broken.

Dialling by colour is required. Most gods can be contacted on red-tipped incense, vegetarian divinities with yellow sticks and spirits via the green ones. The lighting of three sticks at a time is required to get through to Buddha.

"Come and get it!"

Coconut Scrub

- The first step towards healing dry skin is a good exfoliating routine. 1 to 3 times per week is desirable.

2 cups freshly grated or dried (dessicated) coconut
2 tablespoons ground turmeric
60 g ground rice
60 ml coconut oil

- Place all ingredients together in a bowl and mix well.
- Standing in the shower, apply the scrub to your body. Thoroughly scub the entire body, giving special attention to the soles of feet.
- Rinse off and pat dry, then moisturise, as usual.
- Caution: You may like to cover the drain with some muslin, or similar coarse cloth, secured around the edges with masking tape to help keep the plumbing in working order.

Walking on pebbles has a charismatic effect on the entire body

Cucumber Mask

· Good for deep cleansing the pores.

Blend ½ a medium cucumber with ¼ teaspoon of good quality vegetable oil.

· Gently pat the mixture on to face and neck. Leave for 15–30 minutes, then rinse off.

Tartar of Yellow Fin Tuna

For the Tartar:
280 g tuna, minced
20 g shallots, chopped
10 g chives, finely chopped
salt and black pepper to taste
40 ml extra virgin olive oil

For the Crab Rillettes:
120 g crab meat
50 g avocado, diced
50 g ginger, minced
40 g shallot, minced
30 g roasted red peppers, diced
salt and black pepper to taste
30 ml mayonnaise
10 ml lime juice

Truffled Soy Dressing:
30 ml truffled olive oil
30 ml soy sauce
30 ml mirin
30 ml rice vinegar
10 ml lemon juice

Garnish:
4 potato gaufrettes
80 g cucumbers, sliced
4 long chives
4 sprigs chervil
5 g togarashi

- Combine all ingredients for the Tuna Tartar in a medium bowl and season to taste. Refrigerate until required.
- Combine all ingredients for the Crab Rillettes in a small bowl and season to taste. Refrigerate until required.
- Whisk together all the ingredients for the Truffled Soy Dressing until well blended. Leave aside until required.
- Arrange cucumbers in centre of plate and spoon dressing over them. Scoop tartar into mounds and place on top of the cucumbers.
- Spoon the rillettes over the tartar, then garnish with gaufrettes, long chives, chervil and then sprinkle with togarashi. Serve immediately.

Serves 4

Grilled Mediterranean Vegetables

For the Grilled Vegetables:
120 g zucchini, sliced
120 g yellow squash, sliced
120 g red peppers, roasted and skinned
120 g green peppers, roasted and skinned
12 asparagus, trimmed
120 g eggplant, sliced
60 ml olive oil
salt and black pepper,
10 g oregano, chopped
10 g marjoram, chopped
10 g basil, chopped
80 ml balsamic vinegar
2 cloves garlic, roasted in olive oil

For the Couscous:
240 g couscous, cooked
50 g capers, chopped
50 g sun-dried tomatoes, cut in julienne strips
60 ml Sherry vinegar
80 ml olive oil
5 g chopped fine herbs
10 g parmesan cheese, grated
salt and black pepper to taste

To assemble:
4 Parmesan Tuiles
10 g chopped chives
2 g black pepper
4 basil sprigs

- Toss all ingredients for the Grillled Vegetables except balsamic vinegar, onto a baking tray. Drizzle with olive oil and season well. Char-grill for a few minutes.
- For the couscous, combine all ingredients in a medium bowl and mix well. Season to taste and reserve.
- Arrange vegetables in a circle around plate, leaving a small space in the centre. Sprinkle chives and pepper over vegetables then drizzle with Balsamic vinegar and extra virgin olive oil. Place a parmesan tuile in the centre and fill with couscous. Garnish with basil and serve immediately.

Serves 4

Parmesan Tuiles

- Heat oven to 165°C. Line a baking sheet with baking paper. For each tuile, spread about 2 tablespoons of grated parmesan onto tray and spread the cheese into 10cm circles. Bake for 8-10 minutes, or until golden brown. Lift hot tuiles over a small bowl and allow to cool.

Char-Grilled King Prawns

For the Papaya Relish:
350 g papaya, diced
200 g tomato, diced
30 g scallions, finely chopped
20 g basil
2 limes, juice only
2 tablespoons finely chopped red chilli
salt and pepper to taste

For the dressing:
30 g seeded mustard
40 ml sherry vinegar
60 ml salad oil
20 ml extra virgin olive oil

salt and black pepper to taste
5 g chives, finely chopped

To assemble:
12 leaves Belgian endive
160 g mixed salad greens
60 g carrots, cut in julienne strips
60 g red onion, sliced
5 g herbs, chopped

16 king prawns
5 ml olive oil
salt and black pepper to taste

- Combine all Papaya Relish ingredients in a medium bowl and mix well. Season to taste and set aside.
- For the dressing. Blend mustard and sherry vinegar together in a small bowl. Slowly whisk in the oils until thick. Add chives and season to taste.
- Place three endive leaves equal distance apart at the top of each plate. Place a handful of salad greens on top, then julienne carrot and red onion.
- Char-grill prawns on a hot grill. Spoon four small mounds of papaya relish on to each plate and place a prawn on top of each mound. Drizzle with some dressing then sprinkle with herbs. Season with salt and pepper.

Serves 4

158

Penne Pasta Salad

For the dressing:
20 g garlic, minced
40 ml Balsamic vinegar
40 ml olive oil
40 g Dijon mustard
20 g fines herbes (chervil, chives and tarragon), finely chopped
salt and pepper to taste

720 g penne pasta, cooked
80 g artichokes, cooked
80 g sun-dried tomatoes, quartered
80 g grilled asparagus, quartered
80 g grilled mushrooms
40 g grilled red peppers
20 g capers

20 g grated parmesan
4 sprigs basil

- In a small bowl whisk all ingredients for the dressing with a fork, until blended.
- Combine pasta, artichokes, sun-dried tomatoes, asparagus, mushrooms, peppers and capers in a medium bowl and mix well. Season with salt and pepper.
- Divide mixture between 4 serving plates and garnish with parmesan and basil. Serve immediately

Serves 4

Gindara in Soy-Mirin, with Shitake Tortellini

100 ml mirin
50 ml soy sauce
50 ml ketjap manis
10 g celery
10 g carrot
5 g ginger

1 kg gindara
30 ml olive oil
50 g shallots, finely chopped
10 g garlic, minced

300 g shiitake mushrooms, cut into brunoise
3 g thyme leaves
350 g baby kai lan
12 wonton skins
1 egg, beaten

- In a small saucepan, heat soy sauce, mirin, thyme leaves, celery, carrots and ginger until reduced by half. Cool.
- Marinate the gindara in the cold reduction overnight.
- Grill gindara until medium. Heat marinade and pour over the fish to marinate for about 5 minutes.
- Heat 1 tablespoon of the olive oil in a pan and fry shallot, garlic, mushroom and thyme until soft, then allow to cool.
- Spoon 1 tablespoon of cold mushroom mixture onto a wonton skin. Brush edges with beaten egg, and place another wonton skin on top; press edges together to seal well. Repeat with remaining filling and dough.
- Cook tortellini in boiling water for 3 minutes. Drain and keep warm.
- Heat marinade while grilling gindara under a hot grill, about 2 minutes on each side. When fish is done, pour hot marinade over to marinate for about 5 minutes.
- Saute baby kai lan in remaining oil.
- Place one tortellini in centre of each serving bowl. Spoon baby kai lan onto each tortellini, then arrange three fillets of gindara around the mound; pour left-over marinade over top. Garnish with some finely sliced and deep-fried ginger, if desired.

Serves 6

Grilled Red Snapper with Asparagus Nicoise

4 red snapper fillets
30 ml olive oil
salt and black pepper to taste

For the Vinaigrette:
100 g tomato, diced
30 g capers
60 g black olives, diced
30 g shallots, finely chopped

30 g Dijon mustard
40 ml sherry vinegar
5 g chives, chopped
salt and black pepper to taste
80 ml olive oil

28 asparagus spears, blanched
10g chives, chopped
2 basil sprigs

- Season snapper with olive oil, salt and pepper; leave aside to marinate.
- For the vinaigrette, combine all the ingredients and season well.
- Heat the grill, and grill fish until crispy.
- Arrange asparagus on plate in a star pattern and place fish on top. Spoon over some of the vinaigrette then sprinkle with chopped chives. Garnish with basil and serve.

Serves 4

Tropical Fruit Infusion

1 fresh pineapple
1 salak
25 g jackfruit
50 g rambutan
225 ml sugar syrup
600 ml chilled water

- Peel fruit and blend together in a food processor.
- Heat sugar syrup and pour over the fruit. Leave to infuse at room temperature, then chill until required.
- Before serving, strain and blend with water.
- Serve in a tall glass, garnished with a slice of pineapple.

Makes 4 servings

Jamu (for females)

- Recommended by the Javanese Royal family and used by the Princess during her period, as it is proven to smoothen the skin, reduce the vaginal secretion and remove body odour.

100 g turmeric
25 g tamarind pulp, seeds removed
1 cup sugar syrup
1 litre mineral water

- Peel the turmeric and place in a blender with the tamarind pulp.
- Blend, gradually adding the sugar syrup until smooth.
- Stir in the mineral water and serve.

Makes 4 servings

four seasons resort bali at jimbaran bay

The Balinese believe that the water surrounding them *symbolises life*, providing nourishment for the *body and spirit*.

Befitting its seaside location along the shores of *tranquil* Jimbaran Bay, the spa features healing applications from the *restorative ocean* including sea-salt crystals, seaweed and marine aromatics. Aspiring to heighten a *sense of well-being*, to rejuvenate and relax, the pursuit of *balance and renewal* is achieved through indigenous treatments combining ocean elements and garden fresh botanicals.

Indulge in a *Sea Salt Scrub*, followed by a Sea Body Wrap of rich seaweed and an *Ocean Bath* topped with a vanilla, coconut and citrus elixir.

The master plan for the Four Seasons Resort at Jimbaran Bay was to attempt to provide an understanding of Balinese *architectural form* and to give the buildings the *elegance* and *delight* found in traditional Balinese architecture. The use of time-honoured *local materials* and building forms introduces guests to the intricate detail of Balinese planning, construction and design. The hotel, which has been laid out as a *series of villages* surrounding the central hotel facilities, incorporates *500 shrines*; each shrine was built by local crafts people and oriented by a local *village sage*. Reflecting the ambience of Balinese culture and rituals, the result allows for a *micro experience* of Bali itself.

This is truly a resort that feeds the spirit.

Balinese Boreh

The traditional Boreh is an exfoliating scrub made from a mix of ground rice and spices. A warming scrub, good for relieving fever, headaches, muscle aches and improving blood circulation.

The Spa at Four Seasons Jimbaran Bay has developed treatments utilising ancient rituals that blend essences of plants, aromas of healing flowers, Balinese and Indonesian herbs and spices into modern–day beauty rituals.

Water feeds the soul just like the hearth of an open fire.

The magic of the hands

Something which cannot be overlooked is that the resort is centred in a fishing village.

The strait which runs between the east coast of Java and the west coast of Bali creates a large natural fish trap; the abundance of the local catch is echoed in the restorative menus.

To support the neighbouring village of Jimbaran socially, economically and culturally, over 80 percent of the hotel staff are Balinese, predominantly from the local area. Fruits and vegetables from local growers are sourced as much as possible, and local dance and music groups, respected elders and crafts people are employed on a regular basis.

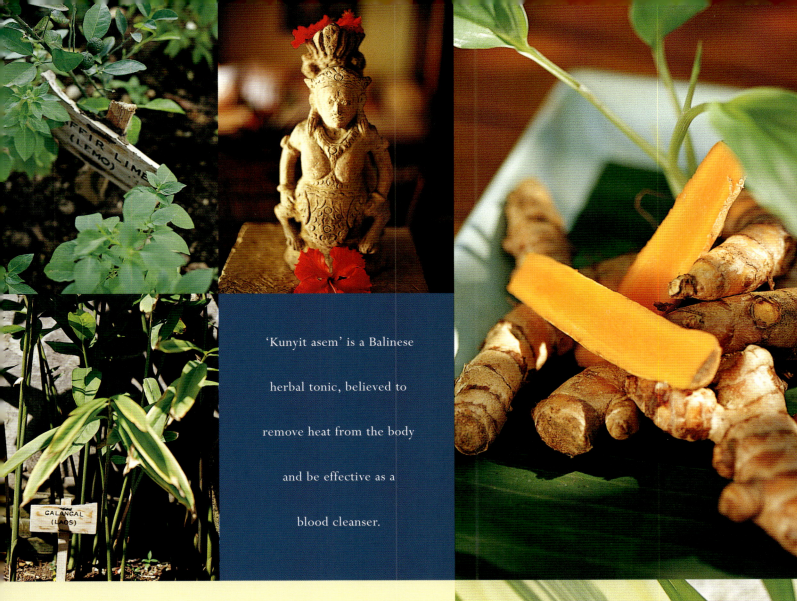

'Kunyit asem' is a Balinese herbal tonic, believed to remove heat from the body and be effective as a blood cleanser.

Jamu Kunyit Asem

100 g fresh turmeric, peeled and sliced
1.2 litres of water
135 ml honey
25 g tamarind paste, diluted with water and strained
65 ml lime juice

- Blend water and turmeric until smooth: strain, discarding the pulp.
- Add honey and bring to a gentle boil. Remove from heat and add lime juice and tamarind.
- Strain again, and leave to cool. Refrigerate until required.

Guava Gulp

120 ml guava nectar	1 raja banana
60 g mango flesh	15 ml lime juice

- In a blender, blitz all ingredients until smooth. Pour into a glass and keep well chilled (perhaps in the freezer) until ready to drink. Garnish with a slice of lime.

Mango Fig and Date 'Energy Bar'

150 g dried mango, chopped	juice and zest of 1 small orange
225 g dried fig, chopped	juice and zest of 1 lemon
150 g dried dates, chopped	1 teaspoon salt
200 ml vegetable oil	250 g plain flour
150 ml honey	175 g rolled oats
80 g brown sugar	13 g baking powder
5 eggs	7 g bicarbonate of soda
1 teaspoon vanilla essence	1½ teaspoons ground cinnamon

- Soak mango, figs and dates in hot water for 5 minutes, then strain, discarding the liquid.
- Add oil, honey, sugar, eggs, vanilla, juices and zests and stir into the soaked fruit.
- Sift all dry ingredients together in a large bowl, then add the fruit mixture, lightly stirring until just combined.
- Pour mixture into a loaf tin, lined with baking paper. Bake in 180°C oven for approximately 30 minutes.

Tropical Passion

120 ml passionfruit nectar
1 raja banana
30 ml sour sop juice
30 ml orange juice
15 ml lime juice

- In a blender, blitz all ingredients until smooth. Pour into a glass and keep well chilled until ready to drink. Garnish with a slice of lime.

Carrot and Low-Fat Yoghurt Muffins

190 g plain flour, sifted	1 egg
140 g wholemeal flour	190 g low fat yoghurt
50 g toasted sesame seeds	85 g brown sugar
15 g baking powder	140 g vegetable oil
5 g cinnamon	50 ml molasses or honey
5 g allspice	375 g carrot, grated
5 g baking soda	125 g raisins
pinch salt	1 litre skimmed milk

- Combine flours, sesame seeds, baking powder, cinnamon, allspice, baking soda and salt.
- Whisk egg with yoghurt, brown sugar, oil and molasses. Stir the egg mixture into the dry mixture until just moistened. Gently fold in carrot and raisins, taking care not to over mix.
- Bake at 180°C for approximately 25–30 minutes.

Charred Rare Tuna in Noodle Salad

120 g tuna loin
salt and black pepper
½ lime, juice only
5 g red miso paste
50 ml Red Miso and Lemongrass Dressing (see recipe)
40 g cucumber, cut in angel hair shreds and soaked in water for 20 minutes
10 g asian cress
10 g tomato, peeled and cut in julienne strips
pinch each of black and white sesame seeds, toasted
½ teaspoon diced red chilli
1 sprig coriander or mint
1 crispy cup, made from fried udon and green tea noodles

- Season tuna with salt, pepper, lime juice and red miso paste.
- Sear tuna in a pan or on a grill, keeping it rare. Set aside.
- Toss cucumber and green salad with Red Miso and Lemongrass Dressing.
- Arrange cucumber salad and crispy noodle cup on a plate with green salad and sliced tuna.
- Sprinkle extra dressing on top of tuna with sesame seeds, red chilli and coriander.
- Serve with a little extra dressing on the side.

Serves 1

Whole Wheat Tagliolini with Mushrooms

15 ml olive oil
30 g mushrooms, quartered
30 g shiitake mushrooms, quartered
10 g garlic, chopped
3 g basil chiffonade
40 g cherry tomatoes, halved
5 ml sherry vinegar
100 g cooked whole wheat tagliolini
½ teaspoon white sugar
salt and pepper to taste
60 g preserved tomatoes

- Heat oil in a sauté pan and sauté mushrooms for approximately 1 minute. Add chopped herbs and cherry tomatoes. Deglaze pan with sherry vinegar.
- Toss in the tagliolini and mix well. Season with sugar, salt and pepper.
- Place preserved tomato on the plate, then arrange the pasta on top. Spoon over the mushroom and cherry tomato mixture.
- Garnish around the mound with mushrooms and tomatoes.

1 portion

Red Miso and Lemongrass Dressing

1 teaspoon chopped coriander
40 ml red miso paste, diluted with water
10 ml lime juice
20 ml light soy sauce
3 teaspoons finely diced red chilli
40 g white onion, grated
35 g lemongrass, finely chopped
20 ml sesame oil
50 ml vegetable oil
1 teaspoon chilli paste

- Combine all ingredients in a mixing bowl and leave to stand for at least ½ hour before using.

Shredded Chicken Salad

100 g poached chicken, shredded

80 g romaine lettuce, shredded

50 g chinese cabbage, shredded

40 g carrot, cut in fine julienne

40 g daikon, cut in fine julienne

30 g wonton skin, finely julienned then fried until crispy

3 basil leaves, torn

3 coriander leaves, torn

40 ml Chilli Mint Dressing

salt and white pepper to taste

5 g red pepper, finely diced

1 g black sesame seeds

1 tablespoon lime juice

Chilli Mint Dressing

75 g palm sugar

100 ml white vinegar

40 ml nam pla

30 g garlic, minced

10 g mint leaves, shredded

5 g coriander leaves, shredded

2 large red chillies, seeds removed and finely chopped

1 prik ki nu chilli, finely chopped

- In a small bowl dissolve palm sugar in the vinegar.
- Add nam pla, garlic and herbs and mix well. Refrigerate until required.

- Toss chicken, lettuce, cabbage, carrot, daikon, wonton crisps and fresh herbs in a bowl.
- Add dressing and season with salt and pepper.
- Arrange salad on centre of plate, scattering herbs around the salad. Garnish with diced pepper and sesame seeds, and serve.

Serves 1

Mediterranean Vegetable Torte

40 g eggplant, sliced and grilled

40 g roasted tomatoes, sliced

80 g zucchini, green and yellow, sliced lengthways

40 g Pepperonata

20 g Caramelised Onions

20 g goat cheese

40 g preserved artichoke, sliced

5 g grated parmesan

3 g basil leaves, shredded

For the salad:

3 g snow pea sprouts

2 g capsicum, finely julienned

5 g sun-dried tomatoes, julienned

5 g mixed pea shoots

10 ml Shallot Dressing

To serve:

20 ml Tomato Vinaigrette

20 g Olive Tapenade

For the Torte
- Combine Caramelised Onion, goat cheese and basil in a small bowl.
- Layer a cylindrical mould with green zucchini, followed with roasted tomato, goat cheese, yellow zucchini, Pepperonata, artichoke, eggplant and sprinkle parmesan on top.
- Bake in an hot oven for approximately 4 minutes, then place under a hot grill for 1–2 minutes to brown.

For the Salad
- Toss snow pea sprouts, mixed capsicum, sun-dried tomatoes and mixed pea shoots with the Shallot Dressing.
- Drizzle Tomato Vinaigrette and Olive Tapenade in a circle onto serving plate. Place the torte in the middle and arrange salad on top. Serve immediately.

Caramelised Onions

2 tablespoons olive oil

750 g white onions, finely sliced

1 teaspoon thyme, finely chopped

1 tablespoon roughly chopped parsley

salt to taste

- Need to give method for Caramelized Onions.
- Place oil and onions in a non-stick pan. Cover and cook over moderately low heat until translucent, about 5 minutes. Remove cover, increase the heat to moderate, and saute, stirring frequently, until onions are browned, about 12 minutes. Season with salt and herbs to taste.

Shallot Dressing

2 shallots finely chopped

60 ml white wine vinegar

½ teaspoon salt

½ teaspoon freshly ground black pepper

½ cup extra virgin olive oil

- Whisk all ingredients together in a small bowl.

Pepperonata

3 tablespoons olive oil

1 white onion, cut in 0.5 cm dice

1 clove garlic, finely chopped

2 red peppers, cut in 0.5 cm dice

2 yellow peppers, cut in 0.5 cm dice

3 tablespoons chopped basil

¼ cup tomato paste

⅓ cup white wine

1½ cups tomato concassee

½ cup water

salt and white pepper to taste

- Heat olive oil in a pan and sauté the onions and garlic until transparent.
- Add the peppers; cook for 2 minutes.
- Add the tomato paste and cook for a further 3 minutes.
- Stir in the white wine, tomatoes and water and simmer until tender and sauce thickens. Season to taste.

Tomato Balsamic Vinaigrette

200 g tomatoes

75 g onion

40 g garlic

50 g celery stalks

50 ml stock or water

60 g tomato paste

250 ml balsamic vinegar

salt and black pepper to taste

- Blend all ingredients together in a liquidizer.
- Check seasoning, and refrigerate until required.

Olive Tapenade

100 g black olives

20 g capers

5 g shallots, finely chopped

3 g lemon zest

3 g thyme, finely chopped

20 ml olive oil

white pepper to taste

20 g tomato, finely diced

- Combine all ingredients together in a bowl, and refrigerate until required.

four seasons resort bali at sayan

Peace – in every sound, every fragrance, every breath …

The Verdant rice terraces and cascading water gardens of Four Seasons Resort Bali at Sayan share the jungle with *ancient shrines*, brilliant heliconias and rugged Banyan trees, encapsulating the *cultural richness* of Bali's mountain region.

Spa treatments are based on the ancient concept of *Ayurveda*, and feature the application of *traditional folk medicine*, which centres on essential oils, massage and meditation to restore the body to its *perfect balance*. This 5000 year-old ancient Indian system of health and rejuvenation places equal importance on *medicine and food* in the care of ones well-being.

Vedic cooking is a culinary philosophy that values nutrition as much as taste in our *sustenance*; we should feed the body which nourishes the *mind and the soul*. This concept comes close to bringing together the culinary wisdom of two major Asian civilisations, Indian and Chinese, but maintains a stronger emphasis on the food fit for the gods like *tonics, elixirs and aphrodisiacs*.

Throughout the resort the *unspoken message* is one of *privacy and peace*. Nature is seen in a balance of earthly and *spiritual perfections*, showcased in the abundant healing elements of the earth. Renewal, found in the secrets of earthen clays, mountain botanicals, warming spices, becomes a celebration of the *healing power of nature*.

Contemporary, yet contextually sensitive.

All paddy fields, trees, vegetables and herb gardens have been kept with buildings blending in or disappearing into the landscape, which includes two rivers and five sacred sites.

Balance between nature and everyday life has been achieved.

Inspired by the world-famous Zen rock garden at Ryoan-ji in Kyoto, the mini Zen garden is a scaled-down representation of nature, with the rocks resembling mountains and the sand, water. Spending a few moments raking the white sands can help calm the senses, clear the mind, and create an ambiance of pure serenity to melt away daily stress.

*Passion–reconnect with your dreams.
Stimulate your neglected senses and
discover untapped energy.
Reconnect with your dreams and find the serenity you seek.*

Guests are encouraged to water and nurture the miniature rice paddies provided in the rooms.

Kecek dancers re-tell myths and legends of yore through dance and drama

Sayan Garden

3 sprigs mint

1 fresh lime, cut in quarters

30 ml sugar syrup

soda water

- Smash the lime and mint together using a mortar and pestle.
- Place in serving glass containing sugar syrup and ice.
- Top with soda water and serve.

Sayan Mary

120 ml tomato juice

120 ml carrot juice

2 dashes Tabasco

2 dashes Worcestershire sauce

salt and pepper to taste

- Shake all the ingredients together with ice
- Rime the glass with salt, if desired. Pour in Sayan Mary and serve immediately.

Crispy Bocconcini with Shrimp and Eggplant Caponata

4 small bocconcini

¼ cup breadcrumbs

salt and pepper

1 tablespoon herbed oil

1 tablespoon olive oil

2 cloves garlic, chopped

½ cup calamata olives, finely chopped

1 each purple, white and green eggplant, diced

15 ml Balsamic vinegar

10 g basil, chiffonade

4 shrimp, cooked and peeled

black pepper

1 tablespoon Coriander Pesto

handful mesclun

herbs for garnish

- Coat the bocconcini with breadcrumbs and fry them in hot oil until golden. Drain.

To make the Eggplant Caponata

- Heat olive oil in a non-stick pan and sweat the garlic, olives and diced eggplant until soft. Add Balsamic vinegar and simmer until reduced. Stir through chopped basil.
- Marinate shrimp with salt, pepper and herb oil then grill.
- Arrange mozzarella, eggplant caponata, Coriander Pesto and mesclun on a serving plate. Place shrimp on top.

Serves 2

Coriander Pesto

1 clove garlic, peeled

15 g toasted almonds

squeeze of lemon juice

1 bunch coriander, leaves only

30 ml vegetable oil

- Place all ingredients, except oil, in a mortar and pestle and grind together to make a smooth paste. Stir in oil. Refrigerate in a sealed container.

Scallop Ceviche in Rice Paper Rolls

500 g scallops, cut in half
20 g roasted red chili
30 g shallot, chopped
10 g kemangi, chopped
5 g lime leaf, shredded
100 ml freshly squeezed lime juice
juice of 1 kaffir lime
4 tablespoons Sweet Sambal
½ teaspoon salt
black pepper to taste
100 g cucumber, cut in julienne
50 g Romaine lettuce, shredded
80 g glass noodles, soaked in water until soft, drained
50 g scallion, finely chopped
50 g red chilli, cut in julienne
200 g enoki mushroom
10 rice paper sheets

- Marinate scallops with all ingredients except rice paper sheets.
- Soak rice papers with warm water, pat dry.
- Place spoonfuls of filling onto rice paper sheets and roll them up.
- Garnish with snow pea sprouts and serve with Sweet Sambal and Tamarind Avocado Dip.
- Makes 10 rolls, cut in 20 pieces.

Tamarind Avocado Dip

150 ml white vinegar
100 ml nam pla
3 red chillies, finely chopped
2 cloves garlic, finely chopped
150 ml tamarind paste
1½ tablespoons sugar
100 ml grapeseed oil
1½ tablespoons honey

- Place all ingredients in a food processor and blend until smooth.

Sweet Sambal

500 g large red chillies, seeds removed
500 g white sugar
1 litre white vinegar
20 g ginger, finely chopped
10 g salt

- Place all ingredients in a saucepan and bring to a boil. Simmer for 20 minutes.
- Leave to cool and store in jars in refrigerator until required.

Note
- This makes a large quantity. Recipe can be halved.

Baby Red Snapper with Spicy Shallot and Tomato Relish

4 baby red snapper fillets or 2 whole fish, cleaned	**6 cherry tomatoes**
	10 lemon basil leaves
4 tablespoons grapeseed oil	**4 small red chillies, finely sliced**
2 clove garlic, finely chopped	**50 g Dabu-dabu Pickle**
	200 g long beans
4 g coriander leaves, finely chopped	**2 whole lime, cut in wedges**
200 ml Dabu-dabu Sauce	

- Season the fish with salt, pepper and chopped coriander.
- Heat oil in a frying-pan. Sear the fish quickly for 2 minutes each side until a golden colour. Then add cherry tomato and cook for a couple of seconds.
- Pour in Dabu-dabu Sauce and hot chilli. Allow to simmer gently for about 6 minutes, until the fish is just cooked. If cooking whole fish allow about 10–12 minutes for cooking time. Add lemon basil during the last minute.
- Serve with freshly cooked longbean and Dabu-dabu Pickle.

Serves 2

Dabu-dabu Sauce

1 tablespoon oil	**2 stalks lemongrass, trimmed to lower 5 cm, and bruised**
250 g large red chillies	
50 g garlic	
10 g small hot chillies	**1 kaffir lime leaf**
10 g ginger	**salt to taste**

- Heat oil in a pan and sauté the chillies, garlic, and ginger until fragrant. Add lemongrass and lime leaf. Season with salt.
- Simmer until sauce thickens a little.
- Remove lemongrass and lime leaf then blend to make a smooth paste.

Dabu-dabu Pickle

1 large tomato, diced	**6 lime leaves, chiffonade**
3 shallots, diced	**2 tablespoons sugar syrup**
2 hot chillies, finely chopped	**2 tablespoons lime juice**

- Mix all ingredients together in a bowl.

Wok-Charred Vegetables with Silken Tofu

100 g silken tofu, cut in squares and deep-fried
50 g baby bok choy
30 g red bell pepper, skin off
50 g onion wedges
50 g zucchini, sliced lengthways
50 g shiitake mushrooms
5 g chopped basil
½ teaspoon salt
¼ teaspoon pepper
1 litre Red Thai Curry Broth, simmering
100 g steamed rice
10 g crispy wonton skin (optional)

- Blanch all the vegetables in boiling water, then refresh.
- Toss vegetables in a lightly-oiled hot wok. Season with salt and pepper, then ad the basil.
- Arrange tofu in the bottom of a serving bowl then place vegetables on top in layers.
- Pour over the hot Red Thai Curry Broth.
- Garnish with crispy wonton skin and fresh herbs.

Red Thai Curry Broth

50 g red curry paste
10 g lime leaves
10 g lemongrass
5 g galangal
½ litre vegetable stock
5 g ground coriander
10 g white sugar
10 g corn flour
1 tablespoon water

- Place all ingredients in a stockpot.
- Bring to a boil, then simmer for 30 minutes. Strain.
- Combine together the cornflour and water and add to the broth, to thicken.

Fire and Ice

2 medium pineapples, peeled, cored and cut in 2 cm slices
100 g white sugar
1 litre water
2 cinnamon sticks
2 pieces star anise
3 green chillies

- Remove the centre core from pineapple slices.
- Boil sugar, water, cinnamon stick, star anise and green chilli.
- Add the pineapple slices to the hot syrup and simmer for 5 minutes.
- Remove slices from the syrup and drain.
- Serve with coconut sorbet.

Coconut Sorbet

500 g white sugar
300 g glucose
1 litre water
1 litre coconut cream
juice of 2 limes
50 ml Malibu liqueur

- Bring the sugar, glucose and water to a boil, then remove from heat.
- Leave side to cool, and when cold, stir in coconut cream, lime juice and Malibu liqueur.
- Chill completely before churning in an ice cream machine.

the ibah, ubud, bali

Head for the hills...

The Ibah in Ubud, is nestled in the *creative gathering* ground of craftsmen and painters from all over the island of Bali. Built at the junction of two rivers in Tjamphuan, the local belief that a *flourish* of *chi* existed in this spot convinced the owners, members of the local royal family, to create this oasis of *tranquility and meditation*.

Stroll through the surrounding small villages where you can see "the real Bali". *Colourful rituals*, *brooding temples* with their *candi bentar* ("gates of heaven") and stone statuary, are every where.

Borrow a mountain bike to cycle along the nearby ridge, white water raft down Tukud Wos, or just settle for the sight of the *white herrons* nesting in the late afternoon at Petulu.

The hosts encourage guests to observe and even participate in the *local ceremonies*, making sarongs and scarves available to borrow, with helpful advice on how to wear them (and how to behave) during the ceremonies at the local temple, Gunung Lebah.

'... the pilgrim, like any traveller, is mostly travelling inside herself, to a destination not found on any map."

- Pico Iyer

The Spa Villa at Ibah, with its warm timbers and flowing fabrics creates an opulent and meditative mood, where relaxation is effortless.

Designed to cater for just one person or a couple at a time, the spa villa is the perfect setting for guests to embark on a rejuvenating journey of sensory awakening and emerge with a feeling of harmonious mind, body and spirit.

Tropical Fruit Crepes

For the Filling:
200 g sugar
10 g cinnamon sticks
10 g lemon rind
3 cloves
400 ml water
100 g pineapple
50 g watermelon
100 g mango
100 g jackfruit
100 g apple
15 g cornflour

For the Crepes:
125 g flour
50 g butter
100 ml milk
3 g salt

- Cook the sugar, spices and lemon rind in the water until a light syrup has formed, then add the fruit.
- Heat briefly then add the cornflour and remove from heat and set aside.
- While the filling is cooling, prepare the crepes.
- Place filling in the centre of each crepe and roll up. Serve with strawberry or raspberry coulis.

Rosewater Stewed Fruit Salad with Yoghurt

70 g apple, peeled, cored and sliced
70 g dried apricots
70 g salak peeled, halved with stones removed
70 g jackfruit
70 g prunes, pitted
2 cinnamon sticks
2 pieces star anise
80 g sugar
60 ml orange juice
1½ teaspoons rosewater
30 g almonds, sliced
100 g yoghurt

- Prepare fruits.
- Place apple and salak in a sauce pan with water and bring to the boil. Cook until soft, but firm.
- Place the sugar, 1 cup of water, the orange juice, cinnamon and star anise in a saucepan and bring to the boil over medium heat. Boil gently for 5 minutes, until a light syrup has formed. Remove from heat and stir in the rosewater. Pour liquid over prepared fruits and allow to soak overnight.
- Serve with yoghurt and sliced almonds.

Serves 3

Tahu Tempe Bacem

4 pieces tofu, 3 cm x 1.5 cm x 0.5 cm

4 pieces tempe, 3 cm x 1.5 cm x 0.5 cm

60 g curry paste

30 ml coconut milk

salt and pepper to taste

Sauce:
Peanut Sauce, Sambal Bajak made from sweet soy blended with chilli and garlic

- Mix curry paste, coconut milk, salt and pepper.
- Coat the tofu and tempe pieces in the seasoning, then char grill briefly over high heat.
- Serve with sauces on the side.

1 Serving

Smoked Marlin Salad

50 g smoked marlin, thinly sliced

5 baby green beans, blanched

3 quail eggs, boiled and peeled

7 baby potatoes, boiled and cut in half

10 g brown onion, finely chopped

4 cherry tomatoes

2 radishes, finely sliced

Sauce:
3 tablespoons yoghurt

1 teaspoon mint, finely chopped

1 teaspoon lemon juice

salt and pepper to taste

garnish with a Pesto Crostini

- Blend the sauce ingredients together well.
- Place all salad ingredients into a bowl and mix together.
- Garnish with cracked black pepper and crostini spread with a little pesto.

Serves 1

Basil Pesto

1 clove garlic, peeled

15 g toasted almonds

squeeze of lemon juice

30 basil leaves

salt and pepper to taste

30 ml vegetable oil

- Place all ingredients except oil in a mortar and pestle and grind together to make a smooth paste; stir in oil. Refrigerater in a sealed container.

Tofu Lime Stir-fry

100 g tofu
4 baby corn cobs
20 g zucchini
30 g long red chillies, seeds removed
30 g daikon
20 g leek
30 g capsicum
40 g carrot
20 g beansprouts
100 ml vegetable stock
15 ml curry paste
15 ml coconut milk
2 kaffir lime leaves

Saffron rice cakes:
40 g Arborio rice
1 tablespoon onion, finely chopped
¼ shiitake mushroom
5 ml turmeric juice (see note)
40 ml vegetable stock
5 ml water
15 ml white wine
1 teaspoon olive oil
¼ leek, finely chopped
5 g fresh thyme leaves
5 g grated parmesan
1 sun-dried tomato
flour for dusting

- Deep fry the tofu until golden brown, then allow to cool and cut into 1 cm strips.
- Cut zucchini, daikon, capsicum, and carrot into batons.
- Heat some oil in a wok and add the curry paste and kaffir lime leaves, stir fry briefly to release the flavour, then add the chopped leek, followed by the baby corn, carrot, chilli, capsicum, daikon, zucchini, and finally the bean sprouts and tofu. Stir-fry for 2 minutes, then add the coconut milk.

For the Rice Cakes:
- Prepare the rice as a risotto, by sautéing the onions and rice stirring continuously, until half cooked. Add white wine, stock and turmeric juice and simmer for a few minutes, then add the shiitake mushrooms, thyme, sun-dried tomatoes and leek.
- Stir in then simmer again. If the liquid has evaporated totally, add water. Cover after stirring and remove from heat. Allow to stand for a minute, then add parmesan cheese. When cooled, shape into balls, slightly flattened and dust with flour. Sear in a pan with olive oil until golden brown.

Three Mushrooms on Rosemary Potato Cakes

Potato Cake:
50 g butter
½ leek, chopped
1 clove garlic, chopped
1 medium sized potato, grated
1 teaspoon rosemary
½ teaspoon salt
½ teaspoon pepper

Three Mushrooms mixture:
1 leek, chopped
1 clove garlic, chopped
50 g butter
2 shiitake mushrooms, sliced
3 button mushrooms, sliced
3 black ear fungi
1 teaspoon thyme leaves
salt and pepper to taste

Balinese Spinach:
1 large handful baby spinach leaves
1 shallot, chopped
½ knob galangal or ginger
1 tablespoon chicken or vegetable stock
1 tablespoon olive oil

For the Potato Cake:
- Combine potato, rosemary, salt and pepper and place in a ring mould in a lightly oiled fry pan. Sear until golden brown.

For the Three Mushrooms mixture:
- Place butter, garlic and leek in a hot pan, when sizzling place remaining ingredients and sauté for 5 minutes over medium heat.

For the Balinese Spinach:
- Place olive oil in a pan over medium heat. Add shallot and galangal and cook until transparent.
- Add spinach and stock and stir over medium heat for 2 minutes and serve immediately.

To make Turmeric Juice:
- Crush a 5 cm piece of tumeric in a mortar and pestle. Drain off juice and use as required.

Salmon Wasabi Ravioli

Ravioli:
15 g smoked salmon fillet
18 g Japanese tofu
10 g sour cream
1 g wasabi
1 g dill
8 wonton skins
2 g coriander leaves

Sauce:
100 ml fish or vegetable stock
10 g capers
2½ g dill
65 ml cream
2 kaffir lime leaves
5 g Dijon mustard
salt and pepper to taste

For the Ravioli
- Finely chop the salmon and tofu, then mix in sour cream and wasabi. When all ingredients are well combined, add the finely chopped coriander and dill.
- Divide the mixture into 8 parts and place in centre of wonton skins, fold skins over and seal with a ravioli cutter. Can be stored in refrigerator overnight or for longer periods in the freezer.

For the Sauce
- Heat the cream and capers over medium heat, until bubbles form. Add the dill and mustard, stir for 1 minute then add the stock, salt and pepper. Serve immediately.

1 Portion

Watermelon, Cranberry and Lime Crush

3 medium sized cubes watermelon
100 ml cranberry juice
30 ml lime juice
15 ml lime cordial
30 ml orange juice

- Place all ingredients in a blender with 1 scoop of ice, and blitz until smooth.

Ibah Iced Tea

500 ml boiling water
¼ cup loose black tea or 4 tea bags
500 ml cold water
to taste sugar syrup, optional
enough ice cubes for 4 serving glasses

1 lime zest only
8 strawberries, hulled and sliced
handful mint
4 strips cucumber peel

- Pour the boiling water over the tea leaves. Stir and leave aside for 5 minutes to steep. Stir again, then strain through a fine sieve; add cold water and sweeten to taste, if desired.
- Fill 4 serving glasses with ice cubes and lime zest, strawberries, mint and cucumber. Pour tea over ice cubes and serve.

alila manggis, bali

"Amazing things happen when you journey to the end of the map"

Escape the crowds and make your way to the unspoiled east coast of Bali.

Wandering off the *beaten path* a little, you will find the area around Manggis offers a *wealth* of culture, natural beauty and outdoor activities. Cycling, trekking, scuba diving, snorkelling and white water rafting are all available there, encouraging you to grow your awareness and *challenge your senses*.

Visit temples and water palaces from *kingdoms past*. Cycle through paddy fields and raft down rivers, observing firsthand the life of the local villagers as they go about their daily activities.

Return from the day's adventure and luxuriate in the airiness of open spaces, simple lines and Balinese touches.

Plan a Balinese seafood barbecue, held in the coconut grove down by the beach, and enjoy local delicacies smoked in coconut husks whilst dancing to *Genjek music*, cushioned by the sound of the rolling waves.

At night, the full moon (Purlana Kelima) rises in the East over the Lombok Straits, *shimmering on the water* and flooding Alila Manggis with *light*.

Breathtaking views of Mt. Agung in the early morning – revere or conquer.

Coffee Scrub

Skin is smoothed and rejuvenated with a stimulating scrub made from aromatic coffee beans are blended with volcanic pumice.

Relax and enjoy some pampering with a spa treatment in your own suite or outside, near the black sand beach.

Deepen the journey and place yourself amongst the locals going about their day-to-day chores. Every third day the market is bigger than usual, and trading is more chaotic; a large moving screen of life and colour amidst the fragrance of fresh produce, smoky incense and fermenting fruits.

Manggis Sunrise

30 ml Grenadine
60 ml pineapple juice
60 ml papaya juice
60 ml mangosteen juice
60 ml soda water
squeeze of lemon
½ cup crushed ice

- Place all ingredients in a blender and blitz until smooth. Pour into a chilled glass and serve, garnished with a slice of pineapple.

Scallop Ceviche

A "cold-cooked" shellfish dish

6 scallops, cleaned
juice of 1 lime
juice of 1 orange
sea salt
freshly cracked white pepper
white sugar
1 small cucumber, seeds removed and sliced into half-moons
1 pink grapefruit, peeled and segmented
1 handful of mint leaves, torn

- Score the scallops lightly with a sharp knife and steep in the freshly squeezed citrus juices for three hours. Drain, and reserve the juice.
- Mix together the juices, salt and pepper, and add a little white sugar to taste. The dressing should taste sweet and a little sour.
- Place the scallops, cucumber, grapefruit segments and mint into a medium bowl and toss in a small amount of dressing. Garnish with a sprig of mint and some finely shredded chilli.

Serves 2

Crab Bisque with Wholemeal Papaya Bread

6 red shallots	**60 ml vegetable oil**
4 cloves of garlic	**1 kg crab shells, broken**
2 stalks lemongrass	**100 ml brandy**
2 small chillies	**2 tomatoes, concassee**
2 slices turmeric	**400 ml chicken stock**
1 lime leaf	**120 ml coconut cream**

- Crush the shallots, garlic, lemongrass, chillies, turmeric and lime leaf to a paste in a mortar and pestle.
- Heat oil in a medium sized pot. Add paste, stirring until fragrant. Add the crab shells, pounding them in the pot as much as possible. When the shells turn bright red, add the brandy. Add the stock and tomatoes, and simmer for 30 minutes.
- Strain through a fine sieve, pushing down on the shells to extract maximum flavour. Bring bisque to the boil and add the coconut cream. Season with salt and pepper.

Serves 2

Papaya Bread

250 g plain flour	**250 g papaya, peeled**
10 g yeast	**8 g salt**

- Combine the flour and yeast in large mixing bowl. Remove seeds from papaya and keep aside. Puree the flesh in a blender, then add to the flour with the seeds and salt. Blend at high speed, until the dough pulls away cleanly from the sides of the bowl.
- Turn the dough ball onto a lightly floured board, and cover with a clean, dry cloth. Leave to rise at room temperature for about 30 minutes. Knead dough again and shape it into small balls, placing them on a non-stick baking sheet.
- Bake 15–20 minutes at 170ºC with a dish of water in the bottom of the oven. Cool rolls on a wire rack.

Poached Fillet of Beef with Kipfler Potato Salad

100 ml olive oil
1 punnet cherry tomatoes
1 sprig of thyme
1 tablespoon red wine vinegar
400 ml chicken stock
handful of celery leaves
2 x 180 g fillet of beef
4 Kipfler potatoes, boiled and skinned
2 cloves garlic, finely chopped
1 teaspoon white truffle oil
sea salt and ground white pepper, to taste

- Heat oven to 180°C.
- In a small roasting pan, heat the olive oil and add the cherry tomatoes and thyme sprig. Add the red wine vinegar and cover with foil. Bake for 15 minutes, then remove and allow to cool. When cool enough to handle, gently remove tomato skins with your fingers.
- In another pot, bring chicken stock to the boil, and add celery leaves and garlic.
- Add beef fillet, turn down to a simmer, and poach gently for fifteen minutes.
- Gently remove from the stock, and allow to rest in on top of the oven until ready to serve.
- Warm the potatoes in the poaching liquid, remove, then toss in the white truffle oil.
- Place on warm main course plate, pushing down hard so they break apart a little. Place beef fillet on top, and the cherry tomatoes. Allow a little of the tomato braising liquid to drizzle over the top and around the plate.

Serves 2

Grilled Squid Salad

150 g squid, cleaned
juice 1 fresh lime
100 g sliced honeydew melon, peeled and sliced
20 g Japanese pickled ginger, drained
100 g mixed lettuce leaves
1 quantity Palm Sugar Vinaigrette

- Score the squid with a very sharp knife making a trellis pattern on the underside of the flesh.
- Pour the lime juice over the squid and allow to marinate for twenty minutes.
- Heat a grill or barbecue and cook the squid until golden brown and slightly crispy. Allow to cool, then slice into bite-size pieces.
- Toss the honeydew melon and ginger with the lettuce leaves, Palm Sugar Vinaigrette, and squid.
- Arrange on a plate, drizzle a little of the vinaigrette on the plate as a garnish.

Serves 2

Palm Sugar Vinaigrette

7 tablespoons palm sugar
80 ml sherry vinegar
5 coriander roots, crushed
3 tsp salt
3 garlic
200 ml vegetable oil

- in a small saucepan, dissolve the palm sugar with a little water over medium heat. Add vinegar, then leave aside to cool.
- Add the coriander root, salt & garlic, then slowly whisk in the oil.

Steamed Salmon in Banana Leaf

1 banana leaf
3 coriander roots
2 cloves of garlic
1 small red chilli
pinch of salt
200 ml fresh lime juice
1 teaspoon white sugar
160 g fresh salmon fillet
steamed rice to serve

- Fill a steamer pot with hot water and bring to the boil.
- Place a heatproof ceramic bowl upside down on the banana leaf. With a sharp knife, cut a circle out, making it slightly larger than the bowl.
- Using a mortar and pestle, crush the coriander roots, garlic, and chilli with the sea salt into a paste.
- Mix the paste with the lime juice and sugar and coat the salmon fillet thoroughly.
- Place the fish and any leftover liquid into the banana leaf, and put into the ceramic bowl. Steam for fourteen minutes, or until medium rare.
- Serve garnished with coriander leaf and rice to accompany.

Serves 1

Pressed Berry and Brioche Pudding

100 ml water
125 g white sugar
200 g mixed berries
1 medium size loaf of day-old brioche
400 ml natural yoghurt
mint leaves for garnish

- Bring the water and sugar to the boil, and allow to caramelise slightly.
- Add the mixed berries, remove from heat and allow to cool.
- Slice the brioche and line the sides of a small ceramic bowl with it.
- Strain and add the cooled berries, top the bowl with another slice of brioche, and weigh down with another bowl, leave overnight. Next day, when ready to serve, invert on to serving plate and garnish with a scoop of natural yoghurt and a fine julienne of mint.

Serves 4

The Chef will proudly take you on a short four-wheel drive through mountainous terrain, to tour the hotel's organic vegetable garden.

Cooking classes are given up here in the outdoor bale, overlooking the peaceful green rice paddies to the Lombok Straits with Mt. Agung in the distance.

alila ubud, bali

*'...seek not to conquer the places you visit,
but surrender to them...'*

From the spacious terrace in your room, inhale the truly *panoramic* views and tranquility of some of the most *spectacular* scenes in Bali.

The Ayung River, as it cuts its *meandering course* through this *magnificent* valley, is watched over by the thatch roofs of Alila Ubud. The breathtaking sight of the mountain and surrounding *volcanoes*, often wreathed in mist or a kind of *curious light*, brings you to the realisation that maybe, just for a moment, *time might be standing still*.

The architecture is a blend of Balinese design and modern geometry. Minutes from Ubud, the hills and valleys nearby contain a number of *traditional villages* and family compounds – *vignettes of a vanishing world*, where travellers with mobile phones mingle amidst incense and village elders, artists and musicians from around the world, who have gathered there to *find inspiration* or keepsakes.

Not-to-be-missed tours include a trip to the island's central *volcanoes*, the village of Kintamani and the beautiful scenery of Lake Batur, a cultural tour of Ubud and a visit to Gianyar, the home of ikat weaving and the *Goa Gajah Elephant Cave*.

On arrival, take time to enjoy a welcome tea in the cabana while absorbing the soaring views of the dramatic emerald-green pool floating above the plunging valley below.

Smiling, caring staff appear from nowhere,

attending to your needs, softening the

linear effect of the stone and wood finishes

The **Ajana** or Third Eye Chakra, is located between the brows in the inward, center of the forehead. Its name means command, perception, knowledge and authority. The **Shiro Dhara** oil flow treatment aims to clear the mind and encourage deep relaxation. It begins with a brief but relaxing Ayurvedic pressure massage. Then, for 20 minutes, a gentle flow of aromatic oil is poured onto the third eye on your forehead. An uplifting and inspiring experience.

Watermelon Lassi

500 g watermelon flesh, seeds removed

2 teaspoons honey

250 ml plain yoghurt

large pinch of ground cardamom

250 ml milk

- Place all ingredients together in a blender and blitz until smooth.
- Pour into a chilled glass and serve.

Wholemeal Fruit Pancakes

1 cup plain flour, sifted
½ cup wholemeal flour
4 eggs
400 ml milk
60 g butter
200 g freshly grated coconut
200 g papaya, cut in 1cm wide strips
200 g mango, cut in 1cm wide strips
ground nutmeg

Coconut Filling:
125 g palm sugar
6 tablespoons water
100 g plain yoghurt

- Dissolve palm sugar in water in a medium saucepan over low heat. Keep 2 tablespoons of the syrup aside. Add coconut to the saucepan and cook for 5 minutes, stirring constantly.
- Assemble the pancakes by spreading 2 tablespoons of coconut filling in the centre of each pancake. Place some papaya and mango along the centre of the filling. Roll up the pancakes and cut in half on a diagonal slant. Arrange 4 pancake halves on a plate and drizzle with some palm sugar syrup, a sprinkle of nutmeg and plain yoghurt on the side.

To make the pancakes:

- Whisk the eggs with ½ the milk then gradually add to the flours to make a smooth batter. Take care not to over whisk as the pancakes will become tough.
- Stir in the melted butter with half the remaining milk, cover and let the batter stand for ½ hour, or overnight in refrigerator.
- Just before cooking, stir in enough of the remaining milk to make the batter the consistency of thin cream, adding a little more milk if required.
- Brush a heated non-stick pan with a little butter and cook the pancakes over fairly high heat, for about 10 seconds on each side. Pile them one on top of the other to keep the bottom ones moist and warm.

Cured Salmon with Slow Cooked Tomato Salsa

720 g salmon fillet
100 g sea salt
50 g sugar
1 cup fresh chopped Italian parsley and basil
black pepper
2 medium sized vine-ripened tomatoes
handful basil or parsley
4 shallots, sliced
2 tablespoons capers, rinsed
8 basil leaves
200 g wild rocket
avocado oil

- Combine the sea salt, sugar, chopped herbs and black pepper and coat the salmon in this mixture. Wrap tightly with plastic wrap and refrigerate for a minimum of 6 hours. Before serving, unwrap and discard any excess marinade.
- Remove the cores from the tomatoes, and place them on a baking tray which has been sprinkled with a little salt. Scatter fresh herbs over the top.
- Bake at 150°C until tender. Cool slightly, then slip the skins off chop roughly.
- In a non-stick pan, heat a little olive oil and sweat the shallots until soft and transparent. Add to the tomato mixture with finely sliced leaves of basil.
- Using a very sharp knife with a long thin blade, remove any dark flesh from centre of fillet. Cut slices from the salmon on a 45° angle.
- Arrange slices of salmon on plate. Top with wild rocket and a mound of tomato salsa. Drizzle avocado oil around edge of plate.

Serves 4

Crab Ravioli with Green Mango & Coriander Salad

240 g crab meat
6 red shallots, chopped
2 scallions, chopped
12 basil leaves, chopped
salt and pepper, to taste
freshly ground black pepper, to taste
12 wonton skins
2 green mangoes, cut into fine julienne
12 sprigs coriander

- In a small bowl, mix the crabmeat, shallots, spring onion and basil and season with salt and pepper to taste.
- Place 6 of the wonton skins on a lightly floured surface. Spoon some crab mixture on to the centre of each. Brush the edges with water and place remaining wonton skins on top, pressing down along the edges to seal them.
- Cut with a round pastry cutter, making sure the edges are totally sealed.
- Combine the mango with the coriander leaves and place in the middle of a plate.
- Blanch the ravioli in salted boiling water until they float to the top. Remove with a slotted spoon and place three on top of each salad.
- Garnish with some extra coriander leaves

Serves 4

Spicy Fish Soup

For the spice paste:
2 cloves garlic
1 small red chili
2 tablespoons ginger
small amount sesame oil
salt and pepper to taste

20 ml ketchap manis
20 ml soy sauce
2 long chillies, sliced
300 g white fleshed fish, flathead, snapper, sea perch, cut in 3 cm squares

For the soup:
500 ml fish stock (well flavored)
2 tablespoons coriander, chopped
2 tablespoons ginger, cut in julienne strips
10 ml mushroom soy
10 ml oyster sauce

For the garnish:
2 tablespoons red capsicums, cut in julienne strips
2 tablespoons tomato, cut in julienne
4 tablespoons coriander leaves
2 tablespoons deep-fried ginger shreds

- Blend all ingredients for the spice paste together.
- In a medium saucepan, place the spice paste and all ingredients for the soup except for the fish, and bring to the boil.
- Poach the fish in the soup for 1 minute, then pour into serving bowls.
- Garnish with capsicums strips, tomato, coriander leaves and deep-fried ginger threads.

Serves 2

Salad of Shaved Chickpeas, Beetroot and Goats Cheese

¼ cup cooked chickpeas

1 small beetroot

100 g goats cheese, roughly crumbled

- Roast beetroot in oven until tender. When cool, remove skin and slice thinly.
- Mix all ingredients together and serve in a small salad bowl with the soup

Snapper Steamed in Ginger

100 ml chicken stock

50 ml mushroom soy

30 ml sesame oil

30 ml Chinese rice wine

1 tablespoon sugar

800 g snapper fillets, cut in 8 pieces

4 tablespoons ginger, julienne

2 large red sweet potatoes, boiled until tender, then cut into large dice

4 pieces baby bok choy

4 vine-ripened tomatoes, sliced in fine julienne

1 clove of garlic

12 basil leaves, chiffonade

2 red shallots, finely sliced

¼ teaspoon sesame oil

- In a fish steamer, combine the chicken stock, mushroom soy, sesame oil, rice wine, sugar, ginger and stir until the sugar is dissolved.
- Bring liquid to the boil and gently steam the fish in it until cooked through, about 15 minutes. Strain liquid and reduce until ½ cup remains.
- Bring a pan of salted water to a boil with the garlic and off cuts from the ginger. Simmer until tender, then drain and toss through sweet potatoes with a little sesame oil.
- In a small bowl, combine tomato, garlic, shallots and basil and season with a little salt.
- Spoon on some of the sweet potato. Place fish on top and garnish with tomato.
- Place the reduced liquid in a small bowl to serve as sauce.

Serves 4

Poached Island Lobster in a Vegetable Nage

4 medium size lobster tails, marron, Balmain bug or anything similar, cut in half

2 long cucumbers, cut in long strands of julienne

2 spring onions, sliced lengthways in thin strips

1 long red chilli, finely sliced

2 tablespoons fried shallots

4 sprigs Thai basil

Vegetable Nage:
1 litre water
500 ml white wine
3 cloves garlic
2 sticks celery
1 carrot, peeled and chopped
5 red shallots
3 leeks, chopped
1 bay leaf
1 tablespoon white peppercorns
1 strip of lemon zest
1 sprig thyme
small amount salt

- For the nage, place all ingredients in a large saucepan and bring to the boil.
- Simmer for 20 minutes, then remove from heat and strain.
- Place lobster into the hot nage and return to the heat. Gently simmer until the flesh is firm but not hard, about 2–3 minutes.
- In each soup bowl, place some of the cucumber, spring onions, chilli and fried shallots. Add the lobster and pour the hot nage into the bowl around the lobster. Garnish with Thai basil and some strips of cucumber.

Serves 4

Seared Scallop Salad with Wakame

200 g sushi rice, washed 3 times

50 ml rice wine vinegar

4 tablespoons sesame seeds, roasted

10 g chives, chopped

250 g tempe, cut in triangular shapes

¼ cup dried wakame, soaked in water

3 scallions, sliced

handful coriander

1 long red chilli, cut in very fine julienne

12 scallops, seasoned with salt and pepper

- Cover the rice with water, 1 cm above the level of the rice.
- Bring rice to the boil and simmer, with lid on, until soft and dry.
- Add rice wine vinegar, sesame seeds and chopped chives. Remove from the heat and let the rice cool slightly in the pot for ten minutes.
- Turn out onto a tray and drag a wooden spoon through the rice to mix, similar to a folding action. Fan the rice to cool it down as fast as possible; doing this will give the rice a nice sheen. While still a little warm, press the rice into a square dish.
- Toss chilli strips in flour and deep fry until crispy. Drain on a wire rack.
- Brush a non-stick pan with a little oil, and when hot, add the scallops, browning them on both sides. They should be still slightly raw in the middle, as they will finish cooking in their own heat.
- Unmould the rice and cut into triangle shapes.
- Layer the tempe, rice and scallops as in photograph, garnish with well-drained wakame, and some extra sesame seeds.

Serves 4

Sentosa Resort and Spa, Singapore

The *colourful* and culturally-diverse *food mecca* of Singapore is more than just an *equatorial* hub for big business and designer labels. With its roots stemming from the Malays, Indian and Chinese, the lion city's *multicultural society* is truly Asian at heart with an *international mind*.

Nestled in the heart of the city, the Amrita Spa in Raffles The Plaza Singapore, is a veritable *oasis* for residents and travellers to *escape* the busy pressures of the outside myriad of *colour* movement and noise. Its name is derived from the ancient *Sanskrit legend* in which, from the beginning of *time*, Hindu deities searched for Amrita, a magical *elixir* that would give *eternal youth*.

Indulge in a Jet Lag remedy, starting with Amrita body polish, stress recovery back and shoulder massage and a mini facial.

Hop a cab to take you across the bridge to Sentosa island – literally minutes away from downtown Singapore but worlds apart from the cityscape and bustling traffic. Spa Botanica is an idyllic green "garden spa" with *invigorating waterfalls*, healing *mud pools* and a labyrinth set up in an intricate design of twists and turns to *relax body and mind*. The galaxy steam bath lets you relax under a *thousand stars;* the steam cloud purifies the skin while the healing mists to *clear your mind*.

Slather your body with volcanic mud, then briefly bake in the sun until the mud dries to a powder. Brush or rinse off in the invigorating outdoor Tsunami shower.

Not to be confused with a maze, the labyrinth is a meditation tool used since ancient times. Walking is a metaphor for journeying into a universe of understanding. Coming back out signifies spiritual and physical awakening.

Beetroot Muffins

1 tablespoon ground cinnamon
½ teaspoon ground ginger
½ teaspoon baking powder
½ teaspoon baking soda
1¼ cups whole wheat buckwheat flour
½ cup wheat bran
¼ cup wheat germ
½ teaspoon salt
1 tablespoon canola oil
½ cup cooked beet root, grated
½ cup plain yogurt
3 egg whites

- Sift all dry ingredients together into a bowl.
- Stir oil, beetroot and yogurt together.
- Combine dry ingredients with wet.
- Heat oven to 180°C.
- Beat egg whites until stiff.
- Fold egg whites into mixture, and spoon mixture into greased muffin pans.
- Bake for 15–20 minutes, until done.

Passionfruit Cocktail

45 ml Jose Cuervo Gold Tequila
30 ml Passoa or Triple Sec
30 ml lime juice
30 ml coconut milk
60 ml passionfruit juice
60 ml pineapple juice

to garnish:
sliced starfruit

- Combine all ingredients and shake over ice.
- Pour into a salt crusted glass.
- Garnish with a slice of starfruit.

Serves 2

Salad of Five Spiced Tuna

240 g yellowfin tuna
2 teaspoons five spice mix
60 g new potatoes
30 g green beans, blanched
20 g mixed greens
4 quail eggs, poached in lightly vinegared water
4 g mixed cress
2 calamansi limes
20 ml fresh tomato puree
3 teaspoons olive oil
1 teaspoon salt and white pepper
2 tablespoons balsamic vinegar
3 tablespoons olive oil
1 teaspoon salt

- Quickly sear each side of the tuna fillet on the grill. Remove, and slice in 1 cm thickness.
- Arrange slices of potato in centre of plate. Layer with 4 or 5 beans, tuna slices and a poached quail egg on top.
- Place a small mound of cress on the side and drizzle the two dressings onto plate to garnish.

For the dressing:
- Blend the tomato with the 3 teaspoons olive oil and season with salt and pepper.
- Whisk the 3 tablespoons of olive oil into the balsamic vinegar until thick, and season with salt and pepper.

Serves 4

Grilled Salmon & Spinach Wrapped in Rice Paper

100 g spinach
2 teaspoons olive oil
8 sheets rice paper
500 g salmon fillet, cut in 4 x 125 g portions
60 g green papaya, shredded
15 g long beans
2 teaspoons coriander leaf
1 clove fresh garlic
2 tablespoons fish sauce
1 birds eye chilli
4 tablespoons Thai chilli sauce

- Sweat spinach in olive oil. Leave to cool.
- Soften 2 sheets of rice paper in warm water. Drain and lay one sheet on top of the other.
- Place salmon and spinach on the sheets and wrap it up like a parcel.
- Place the coriander, bird's eye chilli, garlic and chilli sauce in a mortar and pound it roughly with a pestle.
- Steam the salmon parcels for 10 minutes. Slice the parcels in two and place on serving plates. Serve with shredded papaya, long beans and garnish with fresh herbs.
- Drizzle some of the chilli sauce around the plate.

Serves 4

Poached Chicken and Shrimps with Mint Pesto

80 g chicken breast fillet, skin removed

4 sheets rice paper

60 g shrimp, cooked and peeled

16 g enoki mushrooms

10 g mixed greens

4 g mixed herbs

1 clove fresh garlic

12 g mint leaves

4 tablespoons olive oil

6 g pine nuts

4 g grated parmesan

½ teaspoon salt and white pepper

- Poach chicken breast in boiling water or stock for 6 minutes. Remove and drain.
- Soak the rice paper in warm water for a couple of minutes. Remove carefully to avoid tearing and lay them flat on clean paper or kitchen towel.
- Place one quarter of the chicken, shrimp, mushroom, mixed greens and herbs on one of the soaked rice papers an roll it up. Repeat with remaining ingredients and rice papers.
- For the mint pesto, blend the garlic, mint, pine nuts, parmesan, salt and pepper together in a food processor until a smooth paste is formed. Serve in a small bowl with the rice paper rolls.

Serves 4

Grilled Tandoori Quail Breast

120 g quail breasts

2½ tablespoons tandoori marinade

80 g new potatoes, peeled

50 g cucumber, peeled and shredded

2 tablespoons yoghurt low fat

4 arugula leaves

- Marinate the quail breast in tandoori marinade for ½ hour.
- Boil new potatoes until tender. When cool slice in 0.5 cm thickness.
- Heat grill, and when hot, grill slices of potato on both sides.
- Grill quail until done about 3–4 minutes on each side.
- Combine low fat yoghurt with shredded cucumber in a small bowl. Season with salt and pepper.

Serves 4

Lotus Root Basket Filled with Tuna Tartare

100 g yellow fin tuna

30 g lotus roots

2 tablespoons water

¼ teaspoon wasabi

12 g creamy goat cheese

12 g spring onions

6 g watercress

- Peel the lotus root and slice it very thinly. Heat oil in a wok and fry them until crispy. Drain on a wire rack.
- Cut the tuna into small cubes.
- Blend the water, goat cheese and wasabi to make a dressing. Mix tuna, dressing and spring onions together.
- Make a small basket out of the crispy lotus root, fill it with the tuna tartare and garnish with the watercress.

Serves 4

Grilled Chicken with Tom Yam Risotto

600 g chicken breast
2 teaspoons tom yam paste
120 g Arborio rice, cooked
8 straw mushrooms
100 g baby kai lan, washed
2 teaspoons olive oil
¼ teaspoon salt and white pepper
4 tablespoons tomato sauce
30 g fresh young ginger, grated
2 tablespoons coriander, chopped

- Grill the chicken breast with the skin on to keep it moist. Just before slicing it, remove the skin.
- Boil a little water with the tom yam paste and add in the rice. Leave aside and keep warm.
- Saute the baby kai lan and straw mushrooms in olive oil and season with salt and pepper.
- Warm tomato sauce and add the ginger, stirring for a couple of minutes for the ginger to impart its flavour. Stir the chopped coriander through the risotto just before serving.
- Place a spoonful of risotto just off the centre of the serving plate. Add kai lan, straw mushrooms and fan slices of chicken breast on top.
- Spoon sauce onto plate.

Serves 4

Tomato Sauce

1kg ripe tomatoes
2 tablespoons olive oil
1 teaspoon salt
1 tablespoon sugar
½ teaspoon black pepper.

- Slice tomatoes in half horizontally and squeeze to remove seeds.
- Place on lightly greased baking tray or baking dish. Drizzle with olive oil, and sprinkle with salt, black pepper and sugar. Bake in a slow oven, 140ºC, until soft.
- Place tomatoes in food processor and puree until smooth. Refrigerate until required.

Carrot, Broccoli and Tofu Soup

225 g carrots, peeled and roughly chopped
80 g broccoli florets
150 g roma tomatoes, peeled and seeded
100 g firm tofu, diced
400 ml Vegetable Broth
5 g tomato puree
100 ml soy milk
5 g basil leaves

- Place all the ingredients, except the tofu in a blender and process well.
- Add soy milk until the desired consistency.
- Before serving, add the tofu into the soup and garnish with basil leaves.
- Serve cold.

Serves 4

Vegetable Broth

100 g leek, washed and chopped
250 g medium onions, chopped
200 g carrots, peeled and chopped
250 g celery stalks, chopped
50 g parsley stems, chopped
5 g bay leaves, broken in half
5 g dried marjoram, crushed
0.5 g dried thyme, crushed
1.2 litres cold water

- Combine all the ingredients in a large pot and bring to a boil over high heat. Reduce the heat and simmer, uncovered for 1 hour. Line a strainer or colander with a double thickness of cheesecloth and set it over a very large bowl or pot. Strain the stock.

Sea Bass Fillet with Spinach and Horseradish

200 g non-fat plain yoghurt

80 g prepared horseradish, or to taste

120 ml olive oil

90 g thinly sliced red onions

500 g sea bass fillet, cut in half

20 ml Balsamic vinegar

6 g pepper

80 g parsley, chopped

400 g large spinach leaves

60 g lemon, quartered

280 g vine ripened tomato, sliced

400 g new baby potatoes, boiled and peeled

30 g red capsicum, cut in fine julienne

15 g fennel

15 g basil

15 g coriander

15 g chopped chives

- Heat oven to 180°C.
- In a small bowl mix the yoghurt and horseradish. Set aside.
- In a non-stick sauté pan, heat the olive oil over medium heat. Sauté the onions for 4–5 minutes until translucent. Lay the fish over the onions, add the wine, and season with the pepper and lemon thyme. Cover tightly and bake for about 10 minutes, or until the fish is opaque and cooked through.
- Sauté the spinach leaves for a few seconds. Arrange on plate. Place the fish in the centre of a serving plate, spoon over some of the onions and cooking liquid.
- Serve with small steamed potatoes and chervil or parsley.

Serves 4

Turkey Hash with Poached Egg and Vine-Ripened Tomato

1 medium eggplant, thinly sliced
600 g ground turkey breast
1 medium onion, diced
100 g red pepper, minced
2 tomatoes, diced
300 ml Tomato Sauce, (see recipe page 240)
1 teaspoon salt
6 poached eggs
300 g steamed rice
1 tablespoon chopped chives

- Steam the eggplant slices until tender.
- In a sauté pan, cook the onion and red pepper over medium heat until onions are soft.
- Add the turkey and cook until just done and still juicy.
- Add some tomato sauce.
- Place the eggplant slices on the bottom of the serving dish.
- Spoon turkey mixture over the eggplant. Top with the diced tomatoes and poached egg. Spoon tomato sauce around and serve with rice, garnished with chopped chives.

Serves 6

Strawberry Smoothie

2 cups strawberry yoghurt
4 fresh strawberries
½ cup strawberry sorbet
8 ice cubes
1 tablespoon fresh lime juice
pinch salt

- Place all ingredients in a blender and blitz until smooth.

Serves 4

Mango Smoothie

1 litre mango sorbet
2 mangoes, peeled and cut in chunks
500 ml plain yoghurt
8 ice cubes

- Place all ingredients in a blender and blitz until smooth.

Stir-fried Chicken with Sun-dried Tomato

300 g boned chicken thighs, skin removed, sliced in strips

50 g sun-dried tomato, pureed

15 ml balsamic vinegar

5 g garlic cloves, crushed

3 g black pepper

30 ml olive oil

100 ml tomato concasse

Vegetables for stir-frying:

50 g red onions, sliced

100 g tomato, seeded, peeled and diced

150 g yellow and green zucchini, diced

80 ml chicken stock

10 g corn flour

10 g basil leaves, chiffonade

30 ml olive oil

700 g steamed rice

400 g sun-dried tomato foccacia bread (cut lengthways)

5 g tomato leaves

200 g cherry tomato, peeled

- Combine chicken, sun-dried tomato puree, balsamic vinegar, garlic, black pepper, olive oil and tomato sauce and leave to marinate for at least 6 hours.
- Stir-fry the chicken in a non-stick pan and add the prepared vegetables. Cook until vegetables are tender.
- Add stock, thickened with a little with cornflour. Stir through the basil leaves.
- Serve with steamed rice and toasted foccacia bread. Garnish with tomato leaves and cherry tomatoes.

Serves 4

Avocado Salad with Citrus and Mint Vinaigrette

1 avocado, peeled and sliced

100 g fennel, thinly shaved

120 g baby spinach leaves, washed

1 medium orange, segments peeled

1 pink grapefruit, segments peeled

50 g sun-dried blueberries

1 large red chilli, finely diced

Mint Dressing:

5 g garlic clove, chopped

1 medium orange, juice only

100 ml extra virgin olive oil

3 ml Balsamic vinegar

10 g mint leaves, sliced

2 g salt

2 g pepper

- Stir all ingredients for dressing together in a small bowl.
- Combine all salad ingredients and toss with dressing. Arrange on a plate, and serve immediately.

Serves 4

Wild Mushroom Strudel

150 g spinach leaves
100 g shiitake mushrooms
100 g portobello mushrooms
200 g button mushroom
40 g sliced shallots
5 g fresh thyme, chopped
0.1 g freshly grated nutmeg
0.5 g freshly ground black pepper
70 g crumbled fetta cheese

7.5 g flat leaf parsley, chopped
25 g fresh bread crumbs
120 g phyllo pastry, in 8 square pieces

Mock Sour Cream
170 g 1% low-fat cottage cheese
5 ml lemon juice
2 ml hot pepper sauce

- Lightly coat a baking sheet with vegetable oil spray.
- Sweat the spinach a large non-stick saucepan over medium-high heat for about 2 minutes, stirring, until wilted. Drain in a colander and press to extract the excess liquid, then chop finely. Set aside.
- Heat the oven to 180ºC.
- In a food processor, combine the mushrooms and shallots and pulse to chop coarsely.
- Heat a large non-stick sauté pan over medium heat and sweat the mushroom shallot mixture, thyme, nutmeg and pepper. Reduce the heat and cook for 10-15 minutes, stirring occasionally, until most of the moisture evaporates. Stir in the cheese and spinach and cook, stirring, until the cheese softens. Stir in the parsley and bread crumbs. Leave aside to cool completely.
- Spoon 1/8 of the mushroom mixture onto the sheets of phyllo and roll it up. Place on baking tray and brush lightly with oil.
- Bake in hot oven for 15 minutes. Serve with the Mock Sour Cream and salad.

Serves 4

Cheesecake with 3 berry Compote

100 g low-fat ricotta cheese
100 g 1% low-fat cottage cheese
25 g non fat plain yoghurt
1 large egg
1 large egg white
2 teaspoons lemon juice
1 teaspoon vanilla extract
30 g confectioner's sugar
3 tablespoons cornflour

1 teaspoon lemon zest
100 ml strawberry or raspberry coulis
fresh fruit or mint sprigs for garnish

Crust:
4 whole graham crackers or 30 g (½ cup) All-Bran cereal

Crust
- Heat the oven to 180ºC. Spray a 23 cm pie pan with vegetable oil spray.
- In a food processor, pulse the crackers to coarse crumbs. Transfer to the pie pan and spread the crumbs over the bottom and up the sides.

To prepare the filling
- In a food processor, combine the ricotta cheese, cottage cheese, yoghurt, egg, egg white, lemon juice, vanilla, confectioners' sugar and cornstarch, and process until smooth. Add the zest and pulse two or three times, just until mixed. Slowly pour the filling into the prepared dish and smooth the top with a rubber spatula.
- Set the dish in a large pan and add enough hot water to the pan to come about half way up the side of the dish.
- Bake in the centre of the oven for 25 to 30 minutes, until the filling is set and firm. Let the cheesecake cool completely in the pan on a wire rack.
- To serve, cut the cheesecake into squares or wedges and serve with the coulis, fresh fruit or mint.

Serves 4

glossary

acidulated water – water to which acid, such as lemon juice or vinegar has been added to prevent discolouration of ingredient, particularly fruit or vegetables.

amchur – dried mango powder. Available from Indian grocers.

arugula – Italian name for rocket. A salad green with long spear-shaped leaves and a spicy bitterness.

avocado oil – oil pressed from the pulp of avocados. Its mild taste is enhanced in salads or used for sautéing vegetables, seafood and chicken.

banana trunk – stem of the banana plant comprising many leaves tightly wrapped one around the other.

carom seeds – ajwain seeds. Look like little caraway seeds and taste like a pungent version of thyme. Available at Indian markets and grocers.

cha plu leaves – eaten raw in Thai cuisine used for wrapping snacks and appetisers called "miang". Also called "bo la lot" in Vietnam, erroneously named "wild betel leaf".

chaat masala – hot and sour Indian seasoning blended from coriander and cumin seeds, dry red chilli, dry mango (amchur) black salt and pepper. Used for sprinkling on salads, fruit, snack foods and grilled and roasted meats.

chilli oil – purchased variety is made from sesame or vegetable oil heated with spicy dried red chilli peppers. Fiery hot, it needs to be used sparingly.

Chinkiang vinegar – black vinegar brewed from malt, glutinous rice and masabeto (black vinegar). Prescribed after childbirth to strengthen and prevent chills.

chive oil – cover chives in a bottle or jar with olive, grapeseed or almond oil and leave to steep for 3 days. Strain or leaves herbs in to give a clean, aromatic flavoured oil.

coriander (pak chi) – called cilantro due to its Spanish origins. Fragrant medicinal herb usually added to a dish just before serving. Ground coriander is the ground seeds of the coriander plant used in various curry pastes; the flavour is very different to that of the fresh leaves.

curry leaves – small almond-shaped leaves give an aroma similar to cumin and aniseed when added to curries, particularly fish curries.

dashi – a Japanese fish stock. Available at Japanese grocers in granule form which is then mixed with water.

drumstick leaf – sour peppery flavour used in curries, soups and blanched and eaten whole as in chilli sambal.

enoki mushrooms (winter mushrooms) – Long thin white stems with tiny heads; grows in clumps. Used mostly in soups, salads and nabemono.

foogath – a dry curry, in which the main ingredient, usually vegetable or fish, is cooked with onions and a little masala.

five spice mix – a traditional Chinese spice blend usually containing a blend of anise, cinnamon, cloves, Szechwan pepper and ginger.

fromage frais (fromage blanc) – Smooth, creamy fresh white cheese, sometimes of almost pouring consistency.

galangal (kha) – spicy aromatic rhizome, pink and yellow in colour has a delicate and earthy ginger flavour.

gindara – Japanese name for black cod, or sable fish.

ginger/garlic paste – blend equal proportions of garlic and ginger in a mortar and pestle. Store in a jar covered with peanut oil and keep refrigerated until use. Avoid the pre-prepared varieties.

grape seed oil – low in cholesterol, a light and aromatic, tart and woody flavoured oil, extracted from the residue of grapes. Often used for salad dressings and sauces. Will not solidify when refrigerated.

Greek yoghurt – firm and creamy variety sometimes made from sheep's milk. I use this most times when yoghurt is called for.

groundnut oil (peanut oil, huile d'arachide) – Can be heated to very high temperatures and therefore is a good choice for all types of frying.

ivy gourd leaf (bai tamlueng, scarlet-fruited gourd) – As the name suggests, leaves are typically tri-lobed with small scarlet fruit and white flowers. Used mostly in stir-fries, pickling and salads.

jaggery – dark, unprocessed sugar derived from various palms or from sugar cane.

tofu – Japanese name for soybean curd.

kaffir lime (magrood) – fragrant variety of lime giving little juice. Skin is thick, dark, bumpy and aromatic. Fresh leaves are used shredded or blended in soups and curries. Leaves can be stored well in freezer. The juice is used by Thai women to prevent hair loss.

kai lan (Chinese broccoli) – has dark green leaves, thick stems and white flowers.

kalamansi limes – small, sour and fragrant lime. Greenish yellow in colour. Juice is squeezed over dishes before serving, and is used mostly in Malaysia, Singapore and Philippines.

kemangi (lemon basil) – delicate citrus flavour, mostly used with fish dishes cooked in banana leaves. Similar to sweet basil.

kecap manis – thick sweet soy sauce from Java. Readily available.

lemongrass (serai) – White bulbous base and long-bladed green stalk are too tough to eat, but inside the pinkish layers of stalk can be sliced finely chopped and sprinkled into salads. Has a distinctive aromatic and greenish lemony taste. Lemongrass juice is also a popular ingredient of traditional Thai medicine.

luffa – a gourd with 10 ridges running from stem to tip, and similar internal structure to it's close relative, the loofah (body scrubber). Sweet and mild in flavour, eaten in coconut curries or stir-fries.

mushroom soy – dark soy with a full rich flavour enhanced by straw mushrooms.

mustard oil – pressed from mustard seed and used in northern Indian cookery. When raw it smells hot and pungent; when heated it turns sweet.

nam pla – one of the most crucial ingredients in Thai cooking derived from brewing fish or shrimp mixed and salt, and decanting the fermented result into plastic bottles or earthenware jars. Rich in Vitamin B and protein, Nam Pla should not be seen as a salt substitute but rather as a variation, so go easy.

new potato – small baby potato with a sweet flavour and waxy texture.

nuoc mam – Vietnamese version of fish sauce, made from salted, fresh anchovies, which is stronger in flavour than its Thai counterpart, nam pla.

opal basil – purple basil.

oscietra caviar – small grains of golden brown sturgeon eggs with a strong, nutty flavour.

oyster sauce – a thick rich dark sauce made from dried oysters and soy sauce. Slightly fishy aroma dissipates on cooking. Must be refrigerated after opening.

pak prang (Ceylon spinach) – thick, rounded red-veined leaves. Grows in water, used in stir fries.

palm honey – A Sri Lankan delicacy, also called kitul treacle or coconut treacle, made from palm sugar.

pandan leaf (screwpine) – long, flat, aromatic leaves used to flavour and colour savoury and sweet dishes. As important in Asian cuisine as vanilla is in Western cuisines.

paneer – a firm Indian cheese, similar to pressed ricotta, usually made fresh at home. Chenna is a crumbly, moist form of paneer.

paw pia or **popia wrappers** – Chinese pancakes, available frozen at Asian grocers.

plantain – a cooking banana which is green and unripe and cooked as a vegetable. Skin is also used, after cooking, as an accompaniment to rice.

raja rasa – red skinned banana, used as a vegetable.

red rice – a glutinous variety grown in Bali, Thailand and Japan.

rice vinegar (komesu) – Vinegar made from fermented rice. Readily available at Japanese grocers.

rose water – the diluted essence extracted from rose petals. used in Indian and Middle-Eastern desserts.

saffron water – used in Muslim cooking to add colour and flavour. Infuse a pinch of saffron threads in hot water until cool.

salak (snake fruit) – these very popular fruit of Indonesia and Malaysia, grow in clusters close to the ground have a brown shiny skin which looks like snakeskin. Flavour is like a sweet-sour blend of banana and pineapple. Unripe fruits are pickled, while ripe fruit is eaten raw.

salam leaves (daun salam) – aromatic leaves used to impart unique flavour to Indonesian curries. no substitute.

scallions – known as spring onions in Australia.

sesame oil – oriental sesame oil is dark amber in colour with a nutty flavour, made from hulled, toasted sesame seeds, toasted prior to pressing. Not used as a cooking medium, but small quantities are added to dishes to enhance flavour.

shallots (hon dang) – Thai red onions, are an essential ingredient of Thai salads, adding to the taste, aroma and appearance of the dish. Sweet and aromatic.

sour sop (sirsak) – member of the Annona family which includes custard apple and durian. The flesh is usually consumed as a tangy drink as the flesh can be too fibrous to digest.

snake beans (yard-long beans) – similar in flavour to other green beans, they may be paler or darker in colour, more pliable and can range in length from 30cm to 1 metre. The bean from which the black-eyed pea is obtained.

snake gourd – bright green, thin skinned and known to grow as long as 2 metres. Light on flavour, it is usually stuffed with spicy meat filling.

straw mushrooms – Asia's most sought after fresh mushroom, are very high in protein. Best eaten before the caps are open as this ensures tenderness. Served in noodles and soup.

sugar syrup (Baume syrup) – a cook's preparation used in desserts, sauces and sorbets. To make sugar syrup add 1 cup of sugar to 1 cup of boiling water and stir until sugar is dissolved. Bring liquid to a rolling boil then immediately remove from heat. Store in a sealed container in refrigerator.

sushi rice – short grain white rice, slightly sweetened and soured with mirin and rice vinegar.

tamarind – brown hairy pods containing a sweet, yet acidic pulp around large brown seeds. Sold mostly outside of Asia as a puree or dried. Added to soups and curries for its fruity acidic flavour, but is also used as a preservative and a meat tenderiser.

tatsoi (rosette bokchoy) – mild flavoured, round small-leafed type of cabbage whose leaves fan out in a circle. Has white leaf ribs and dark leaf edges. Used in stir-fries and soups.

tempeh – tofu which has been fermented with a mould and formed into a chunky soy bean cake. Sliced then fried, steamed or baked, it is high in vitamins, especially B12 and has a nutty, smoky flavour.

Thai basil (holy basil or kapow) – used in Thailand and Vietnam. Dark green leaves with purple or green centres. Pungent and aromatic rather than sweet. Planted outside temples, it is said to repel insects.

tobiko – flying fish roe available in orange, red and green colours.

togarashi – Japanese name for chilli. Can refer to fresh or ground chilli.

tomato concassee – tomatoes which have been peeled, seeded and diced. Peeling tomatoes is easily achieved by making a few knife slashes into the tomato skin, plunging them into boiling water for about 5 seconds, then into iced water for 30 seconds. The skin will peel off easily. Cut the tomato accross the centre (equator) of the tomato and squeeze out the seeds. Dice and drain the tomatoes, then use as required.

turmeric (khamin) – thin, brown-skinned root of the ginger family has an iridescent bright orange interior that stains anything it touches. Particularly popular in southern Thailand where curries are more fiery than elsewhere in the country.

urad dhal (blackgram dhal) – a pulse sold with its black skin on, or husked, leaving it creamy white in colour.

wakame – seaweed mainly used in miso soup, salads and sushi. Available outside of Japan in its dried form.

wasabi – grown as a root and freshly grated, or in its powdered form, is made into a pale green paste by mixing with a little water. Available as a powder, or a paste which is sold in tubes.

white mushroom soy – soy with a full rich flavour enhanced by shiitake mushrooms.

yam noodle (shirataki) – thin, soft noodles of konnyaku, or elephants foot. An essential ingredient of sukiyaki.

yellow miso paste – shiro miso paste, sometimes called white miso, although it is yellow in colour. Mild in flavour, it is used in soups, marinades and white fish dishes.

The journey is only half over once you get home....

Analyse your eating, exercise and relaxation habits and identify areas for improvement. Here are some tips you may find useful to help keep the momentum going and make any necessary changes on your return.

Exercise
Start slowly.
Get stretching and gain flexibility. Aiming at 30-45 minutes of exercise each day is a good goal to begin with. Always remember to stretch for 5 minutes after any exercise.
If you're trying to lose weight, diet alone just won't cut it and you'll end up losing muscle along with fat. Exercise enables you to maintain your muscle tone by increasing metabolism as you lose fat.

Start the day with a brisk 30 minutes walk on a designated walking track or around an oval, so that without fear of traffic you can practice my favourite Tibetan buddhist trick and concentrate on the moment. Instead of letting your mind wander about meetings and conversations, take in the surroundings, enjoy the mindlessness. .. and breathe.

Motivation can be the problem for most of us.
Set goals and reward yourself when you meet them with a movie or a pedicure.
If you haven't already, make a habit of walking the dog. You don't want to let someone else down, as well as yourself.

Share the experience.
Some of us need a buddy to help us attain goals beyond our own expectations. If this is you, hire a personal trainer, enlist a friend or join a class. Get to know the other like-minded people there and let their enthusiasm and energy inspire you to stick to healthy ways.
Don't ignore the instructors in the gym; make friends with them and don't be afraid to ask for their assistance and tips.

Having your gym bag packed the night before can help you overcome those early morning moments of procrastination. Unlace the gym shoes and place the running gear by the bedside, if that helps.

Maintenance is the key.
Once you make a series of small changes to your daily routine, you feel the results in immeasurable ways. But don't be too confident about sticking to the new schedule; write it into your diary so that you feel accountable and less likely to skip a session. Try different kinds of workouts so that you don't become bored, and remember, patience pays off.

Create a spa ambience in your bathroom at home and make it a sanctuary of relaxation, detoxification and rejuvenation.
Warm baths are best, as water that is too hot will over-stimulate your senses.
Shut the door- keep those unwanted distractions out and all the good vapours in.

Soothing music can relieve stress, lower blood pressure and even ease pain, whilst upbeat music encourages the brain to release mood-improving endorphins. Singing is known to relieve stress by causing relaxing vibrations in the throat. Laughter boosts immunity, strengthens hearts and improves lung function. Humour inspires creativity, reduces stress and bolsters mental health.

Accept the importance of having a good nights sleep.
Give your body time to slow down before trying to drop off to sleep. A few drops of lavendar oil on the pillow or in a warm bath before bedtime, can have a soporific effect.

Eat lightly at night, and avoid caffeine-laden beverages. If possible, set a curfew on food so that you avoid eating 3-4 hours before bedtime.

By keeping simple flavours in balance it is easy to produce wholesome, flavoursome food that nourishes body and soul. Look for the purity in the absolute freshness of ingredients.
Always eat slowly as it takes 20 minutes for your stomach to send signals to your brain that you are full.

Hydration combats stresses such as fatigue, tiredness, headaches, lack of focus, digestive problems and nervousness. Drinking fluids throughout the day will keep your body cleansed by flushing out toxins and increasing the body's ability to absorb minerals and nutrients.

Small dietary changes can make a big dent in your fat and sugar intake, so have fruit for dessert.

Whilst all types of alcohol are known to reduce HDL cholesterol, the good one, by releasing antioxidant vitamins, we can achieve an adequate intake of the same polyphenols by eating plenty of fruit, vegetables and drinking tea.
Alcohol is the most common cause of insomnia, so limit your intake. 1-2 small glasses a day can calm you down after a hard day, but any more will send you off to sleep, only to wake you a couple of hours later.

Meditation doesn't need to be transcendental to be beneficial. Sit in a quiet place where you won't be interrupted, and concentrate on your breathing. Light a candle to give yourself an object of focuses. When thoughts break through the calm, just let them come and go. After 15 minutes sit quietly for a few minutes more before getting on with the day or the good nights sleep ahead.

Pare down - make your life as uncluttered in as many ways as you can.
Cut the cord with the cellphone - dependence can be similar to that of other substances. Spend a couple of minutes each day doing absolutely nothing - just be.

Yoga and meditation are the best tools I use to relax and find a peace that may not be attainable from external or materials things. As well as achieving defined muscle tone, vibrant health and energy, I can feel, think and see things from a new perspective.

Learn to think positive thoughts - you'll be able to cope with anything. A little positive rebalancing at night will allow your subconscious to soak it up while you sleep. Negative thoughts drain your energy, as do negative people. If necessary, remove the altogether and make space for more positive ones.

recipe index

Ahi Tuna Loin	45	Goi Cuon	60	Passionfruit Cocktail	237	Squid with Red Curry	85
Asian Minestrone	79	Grape Terrine	83	Paw Pia Soot	105	Steamed Custard in Pumpkin	69
Asiatic Pennywort Cocktail	100	Green Mango Salad	93	Penne Pasta Salad	158	Steamed Plantain	32
Avocado Salad	243	Grilled Chicken Pepperonata	107	Pineapple and Mint Smoothie	142	Steamed Salmon in Banana Leaf	218
Baby Red Snapper	191	Grilled Red Snapper with		Plain Uthappam	30	Steamed Snapper in Ginger	230
Baked Chicken Breast	128	Asparagus Nicoise	159	Poached Chicken and Shrimp		Steamed Snapper	
Banana and Coconut Foogath	29	Grilled Mediterranean Vegetables	157	with Mint Pesto	239	with Vegetables	107
Banana Trunk in Mild Spice	29	Grilled Skinless Chicken Breasts	238	Poached Chicken Roulade	45	Stir-Fried Chicken	243
Beef Pho	58	Grilled Squid Salad	217	Poached Fillet of Beef	217	Strawberry Salad	146
Beef Stock	58	Grilled Salmon and Spinach		Poached Island Lobster	231	Strawberry Smoothie	242
Beetroot Muffins	237	in Rice Paper	238	Poached Salmon with Lime	95	Sushi Kaow Soy	133
Beetroot Salad	230	Grilled Tandoori Quail Breast	239	Pomelo and Prawn Salad	68	Sweet Sambal	190
Bircher Muesli	78	Guava Gulp	174	Prawn Congee	58	Sugar Pea Soup	41
Boiled Red Rice	25	Home-made Yoghurt	41	Prawn and Gazpacho Salad	43	Sweet and Sour Fish	69
Caesar Salad with Beef	83	Ibah Iced Tea	205	Prawn and Kachumbar Salad	26	Szechwan Orange Chicken	
Cajun Tuna Loin	42	Iced Pineapple and		Pressed Berry and		Tahu Tempe Bacem	201
Cameron Highlands Strawberries	146	Aniseed Mousse	121	Brioche Pudding	218	Tamarind Chutney	32
Carpaccio of Tuna	115	Jamu (for females)	160	Pumpkin Soup	82	Tandoori Reef Fish	35
Carrot, Broccoli and Tofu Soup	240	Jamu Kunyit Asem	173	Pumpkin Risotto	144	Tandoori Chicken and Pineapple	26
Carrot and Uthappam	30	Julienne Vegetable Salad	59	Raita	32	Tartar of Yellow Fin Tuna	157
Carrot and Yoghurt Muffins	174	Kaeng Pah Jay	94	Rice and Pickled Lime Broth	25	Thai Apple-Celery Salad	79
Chaat Dressing	32	Kaow Phod Poo	93	Rosemary Potato Cakes	202	Thai Style Barbecue Chicken	95
Char-Grilled King Prawns	158	Kaow Kluk Kapi	132	Rosewater Stewed Fruit	200	Three Mushrooms on	
Charred Rare Tuna Noodle Salad	175	Lemongrass Sunrise	92	Saffron Yoghurt	32	Tofu Lime Stir-Fry	202
Cheesecake with 3 Berry Compote	244	Lemongrass Tea	61	Salad of 5-Spice Tuna	238	Tomato Chutney	32
Chicken Tea Soup with Shark Fin	134	Lemongrass Yam Noodle Salad	94	Salmon Wasabi Ravioli	204	Tomato Rasam	25
Chickpea Curry	32	Lentil and Drumstick Leaf Soup	25	Sashimi Tuna	106	Tomato Tartare with Green Beans	144
Chilli Mint Dressing	176	Lentil Salad	43	Sauteed Chicken Livers	128	Tom Gai Prung	71
Cleansing Cocktail	68	Lobster with Green Apple and		Sayan Garden	189	Tom Yaam Pla Nam Sai	102
Clear Vegetable Soup	133	Avocado	42	Sayan Mary	189	Tropical Fruit Crepes	200
Coconut Chutney	30	Maharaja Kebabs	34	Scallop Ceviche	216	Tropical Fruit Infusion	160
Corn Soup with Crab meat	93	Manggis Sunrise	215	Scallops with Wakame,		Tropical Passion	174
Crab Bisque	216	Mango with Chilli and Salt	61	Lime and Coriander	115	Tuna Parfait with Two Caviars	116
Crab Ravioli	229	Mango, Fig and Date Energy Bar	174	Seabass Fillet with Spinach		Tuna Tartar in Lotus Root Basket	239
Crispy Bocconcini with Shrimp	189	Mango Lassi	27	and Horseradish	241	Turkey Hash	240
Crispy Skin Red Snapper	44	Mango, Pineapple and Orange		Seafood Omelette	59	Vegetable Terrine	82
Cured Salmon	228	Cooler	61	Seafood Hotpot	60	Yaam Polomai	70
Curried Yoghurt and Plantain	29	Mango Smoothie	242	Seared King Prawn with		Yaam Thua Pu	71
Datai Punch	142	Marinated Beef on Drunken Rice	117	Gazpacho Salad	43	Watermelon, Cranberry and Lime	204
Demi-Glace	128	Masala Lassi	27	Seared Scallop Salad	231	Watermelon and Fennel Quencher	61
Eggplant Salad	106	Masala Uthappam	30	Sesame Spinach	117	Watermelon Lassi	227
Egg White Omelette	78	Mediterranean Vegetable Torte	178	Sesame Sweet Potato	117	Wholemeal Fruit Pancakes	228
Fire and Ice	192	Millefeuille of Crab	43	Shredded Chicken Salad	176	Wholewheat Tagliolini	175
Fresh Coconut Milk	35	Mint Yoghurt	32	Smoked Marlin Salad	201	Wild Mango Sorbet	47
Fresh Complexion	68	Miso Broth with Tatsoi-Enoki Salad	115	Snow Pea Soup	31	Wild Mushroom Strudel	244
Fruit Loaf	174	Mushroom Herb Omelette	101	Soy Pancakes with Apricot Sauce	101	Wok-Charred Vegetables	192
Gaang Hin Yang	70	Mushroom Risotto	116	Spiced Uthappam	30		
Gado-Gado	143	Narm Prig Noom	92	Spicy Fish Soup	229		
Gang Lieng Goon	134	Onion and Beetroot Akchar	32	Spicy Jungle Curry	94		
Gazpacho Andalusia	142	Orange, Mango and		Spicy Mushroom Salad	131		
Germ Warfare	68	Pineapple Smoothie	142	Spicy Wing Bean Salad	132		
Gindara in Soy-Mirin	159	Oven Roasted Cod Fillet	118	Spicy Yoghurt	29		
Ginger Tea	56	Papaya Bread	216	Spinach Citrus and Sprout Salad	27		

spa directory

The Maldives

Malé International Airport is served by a number of international and charter airlines.

Contact your local Embassy for visa requirements.

Weather
Like many tropical locales, The Maldives experience a dry season, or iruvai, from December through March, and a wet season, known as hulhangu, from May to November. Seasonal transitions in mid-April and late November are typically very calm, producing exceptionally clear seas. The daily high temperature is consistent at 30°C (86°F) year-round, but tropical sea breezes make the warm temperature quite pleasant.

Four Seasons Maldives

North Malé Atoll,
Republic of Maldives
Tel: 960 444 888
Fax: 960 441 188
Website: www.fourseasons.com

How to get there to Kuda Huraa
Guests are met by Four Seasons staff at the Malé International Airport on the island of Huhule and walked to a waiting speedboat for the 25 minute speedboat ride to get to Kuda Huraa, which is approximately 20 kilometres (12 miles) from Huhule.

Consult your local consulate for visa requirements.

Hong Kong

Hong Kong International Airport is served by a large number of international and charter airlines.

Contact your local PRC Embassy for visa requirements.

Weather
Hong Kong's high season, October through late December, is popular for a reason: the weather is pleasant, with sunny days and cool, comfortable nights. January, February, and sometimes early March are cold and dank, with long periods of overcast skies and rain. March and April can be either cold and miserable or sunny and beautiful. By May the temperature is consistently warm and comfortable.

June through September is typhoon season, when the weather is hot, sticky, and very rainy.

InterContinental Hong Kong

18 Salisbury Road, Tsimshatsui,
Kowloon, Hong Kong
Tel: 852-2721 1211
Fax: 852- 2739 4546
www.ichotelsgroup.com

How to get to InterContinental Hong Kong
InterContinental Hong Kong, with its unique and convenient Kowloon waterfront location, offers unrivalled views of Victoria Harbour and Hong Kong Island, and unparalleled service and facilities. 0km to downtown Tsim Sha Tsui

The hotel is 36 km/22.37 ml SE from Chek Lap Kok International Airport (HKG). The resort operates its own airport transfer service.

A 45 minute taxi ride will cost around HK $400.00 or 30 minutes by train will ccst HK $180

Vietnam

Ho Chi Minh City and Hanoi International Airports are served by a large number of international and charter airlines.

Contact your local Vietnam Embassy for visa requirements.

Weather
The influences of monsoons, typhoons and of the complicated topography in Vietnam, the climate is always varying from year to year. However the weather patterns affecting Nha Trang are much more settled with an average daily temperature 26°C and humidity usually arcund 80%.

In general, South Vietnam has two seasons, a hot and rainy season from May to October, and a cold season from November to April.

Ana Mandara Resort, Nha Trang

Beachside Tran Phu Blvd, Nha Trang, Vietnam
Tel: 84 58 829 829
Fax: 84 58 829 629
e-mail: reservations-anamandara@evasonresorts.com
http://www.sixsenses.com

How to get to Ana Mandara Resort
Located on the beach on dramatic Ninh Van Bay, off the famous thoroughfare, Tran Phu Boulevard, the resort rests comfortably on 20,000 square meters of private tropical gardens overlooking the sea. It is 450 kilometres away from Ho Chi Minh City and 1275 km from Hanoi, the Capital of Vietnam. Conveniently located 2 kms from Nha Trang town center and a few minutes by car from the airport. The resort operates its own airport transfer service.

Thailand

Bangkok International Airport is served by a large number of international and charter airlines. Contact your local Thai Embassy for visa requirements.

Weather
Thailand's three seasons run from hot (March through May) to rainy (June through September) to cool (October through February). Humidity is high all year, especially during the hot season. The cool season is pleasantly warm in Bangkok, and is the peak season. Daily temperature averages are in the 30's.

Bangkok Marriott Resort & Spa

257 Charoennakorn Road, Samrae Thonburi
Bangkok, 10600 Thailand
Tel: 66 2 4760022
Fax: 66 2 4761120
Website: http://marriott.com

How to get to the Bangkok Marriott Resort & Spa
36 km North of Bangkok International Airport, Bangkok. Estimated taxi fare: 12 USD (one way)

The Bangkok Marriott Resort & Spa is located on the Thonburi side of Bangkok's Chao Phraya River, away from the congestion of business and large hotels. Nestled on 11 acres of lush gardens, pools and lily ponds it is Bangkok's only riverside resort.

The Oriental Bangkok

48 Oriental Avenue
Bangkok 10500
Thailand
Telephone: 66 2 659 9000
Facsimile: 66 2 659 0000
Website: https://www.mandarinoriental.com

How to get to the Oriental Bangkok
30 minute taxi ride from Bangkok Airport to the hotel is approximately USD 25. Hotel limousine transfer is available: The airport bus takes 1 hour and helicopter takes 10 minutes.

The Oriental Bangkok has an unrivalled river position on the Silom side of the Chao Praya.

spa directory

Hua Hin

Hua Hin airport has commuter service from Bangkok's domestic terminal, and also accepts private planes and helicopters.

Weather
The climate in Central Thailand is ruled by monsoons that produce three seasons. March–June is the Hot Season, July–October is the Rainy Season with the heaviest rains falling from August onwards. Throughout both of these seasons the temperatures average 28°C.

November–February is the Cool Season, with average daily temperatures of 26°C, and overnight temperatures dropping to 13°C.

Chiva Som

73/4 Petchkasem Road, Hua Hin,
Prachuab Khirikham 77110,
Thailand.
Tel: 66 32 536 536
Fax: 66 32 511 154
e-mail: reservation@chivasom.com
Website: http://www.chivasom.com

How to get to Chiva Som
The journey by car from Bangkok Airport to the warm welcome of Chiva-Som takes less than 3 hours. Limousines are available for this journey.

Flight time from Bangkok Airport to Hua Hin Airport is 40 minutes. Pick up from Hua Hin Airport is by Resort Van.

Evason Hua Hin Resort

9/22 Moo 5 Parknampran Beach, Pranburi
Prachuab Khiri Khan, 77220, Thailand
Tel: 66 32 618 200
Fax: 66 32 618 201
e-mail: reservations-huahin@evasonhideaways.com
Website: http://www.sixsenses.com

How to get to Evason Hua Hin Resort
The resort is located at Pranburi approximately 23 kilometres south of Hua Hin town and 230 kilometres southwest of Bangkok. Traveling time by car from Hua Hin town is 30 minutes, from Bangkok approximately three hours.

A 30-minute flight from Bangkok International Airport can be booked directly with the resort. Complimentary transfers between the Hua Hin Airport meet all incoming flights.

Chiang Mai

Chiang Mai is easily accessible from Bangkok International Airport, with numerous flights departing daily. The flight time from Bangkok is only 55 minutes. There are also several direct flights to Chiang Mai from neighbouring countries, including Japan, Bangladesh, China, Taiwan, Myanmar, Laos and Singapore.

Weather
Northern Thailand has three distinct seasons. November to February is the cooler season. During these months it is comfortably warm during the day, with cool evenings and a relatively low humidity. Temperatures generally range from 13°C to 31°C (56°F to 90°F). March to May is the summer season, with temperatures ranging from 17°C to 36°C (63°F to 97°F). June to October is warmer, with higher humidity, short tropical showers and a daily temperature in the range of 21°C to 32°C (70°F to 90°F).

Four Seasons Chiang Mai

Mae Rim-Samoeng Old Road, Mae Rim
Chiang Mai Thailand 50180
Tel: 66 53 298 181
Fax: 66 53 298 190
Website: www.fourseasons.com

How to get to Four Seasons Chiang Mai
30 minutes by car from Chiang Mai international Airport. The resort operates its own airport transfer service.

Phuket

Phuket is served by numerous domestic and regional flights, and Bangkok, less than two hours flying time away, has connections to major international destinations.

Weather
The dry season in Phuket extends from November to April. The rainy season is between May and October. While there can be frequent showers during the rainy season, these tend to be of short duration and are often followed by sunshine. Temperatures year-round range from 21°C to 35°C (70°F to 90°F). Water temperatures are always a pleasant 25°C to 28°C.

Amanpuri

Pansea Beach, Phuket 83000, Thailand
Tel: 66 76 324 333
Fax: 66 76 324 100
e-mail: amanpuri@amanresorts.com
http://www.amanresorts.com

How to get to Amanpuri
A 25-minute, scenic drive from the airport through rice fields, small villages and rubber plantations will bring you to Amanpuri.

Complimentary private limousine transfers to and from Phuket airport are offered to guests and the 17km drive takes 25 minutes.

Evason Phuket Resort and Spa

100, Vised Road,
Tambon Rawai, Muang District,
Phuket 83130, Thailand
Tel: 66 76 381 0107
Fax: 66 76 381 018
e-mail: reservations-phuket@evasonresorts.com
http://www.sixsenses.com

How to get to Evason Phuket Resort
Travelling time from Phuket Airport is approximately 55 minutes. The resort operates its own airport transfer service.

Malaysia

Kuala Lumpur International Airport is served by a large number of international and charter airlines. Contact your local Malaysian Embassy for visa requirements.

Weather
Malaysia's equatorial climate is fairly uniform throughout the year; temperatures range from the low 30s during the day to low 20s at night. The mountains may be 5° cooler than the lowlands. Relative humidity is usually about 90%. Rain is common all year, yielding brief showers. A rainy season brought on by monsoons lasts from November through February on the east coast of the peninsula.

The Datai

Jalan Teluk Datai, 07000 Pulau Langkawi,
Kedah Darul Aman, Malaysia
Tel: 60 4 959 2500
Fax: 60 4 959 2600
e-mail: datai@ghmhotels.com
For reservations contact the website:
www.ghmhotels.com

spa directory

How to get to the Datai
Domestic flights are scheduled daily to Langkawi Airport from Kuala Lumpur and Penang, while international flights come in from Singapore and London twice weekly.

The resort operates its own airport transfer service. The Datai is 30 minutes by car from the island's international airport, which is 20 kilometers west of Pulau Langkawi's main town, Kuah.

Indonesia

Ngurah Rai International Airport at Denpasar is served by a number of international and charter airlines.

Contact your local Indonesian Embassy for visa requirements.

Weather
Bali enjoys comfortably warm temperatures (averaging 27°C/81°F) with cool mountain air and relatively low humidity from April to October. The rainy season, from November to March, brings short bursts of rain interspersed with brilliant sunshine, warmer temperatures (32°C/90°F) and higher humidity.

The Legian Bali

Jalan Laksmana, Seminyak Beach
Bali 80361
Indonesia
Tel: 62 361 730 622
Fax: 62 361 730 623
e-mail: legian@ghmhotels.com
Website: ww.ghmhotels.com

How to get to the Legian
The Legian is situated on Bali's southern coast, in the peaceful district of Seminyak, and is a mere 20 minute drive from Ngurah Rai International Airport. The resort operates its own airport transfer service.

Four Seasons Jimbaran Bay

Jimbaran, Denpasar, Bali
Indonesia 80361
Tel: 62 361 701010
Fax: 62 361 701020
Website: www.fourseasons.com

How to get to get to Four Seasons at Jimbaran Bay
The Resort is only a 15-minute drive from Ngurah Rai International Airport in Denpasar. The resort operates its own airport transfer service.

Ubud

Four Seasons Sayan

Sayan, Ubud, Gianyar 80571 Bali
Indonesia
Tel: 62 361 977577
Fax: 62 361 977588
Website: www.fourseasons.com

How to get to Four Seasons at Sayan
The Resort is a one-hour drive (35 kilometres or 22 miles) from Ngurah Rai International Airport in Denpasar. The resort operates its own airport transfer service.

Ibah

Ibah Luxury Villas
Campuhan, Ubud, Bali
Postal address: PO Box 193, Ubud, Bali, Indonesia
Tel: 62 361 974466
Fax: 62 361 974467
e-mail: sales@ibahbali.com

How to get to Ibah
A few minutes drive from central Ubud. The resort operates its own airport transfer service.

Alila Ubud

Desa Melinggih Kelod
Payangan, Gianyar 80571, Bali
Indonesia
Tel: 62 361 975 963
Fax: 62 361 975 968
e-mail: ubud@alilahotels.com

How to get to Alila Ubud
A few minutes drive from central Ubud. The resort operates its own airport transfer service.

Manggis

Alila Manggis

Buitan, Manggis
Karangasem 80871, Bali
Indonesia
Tel: 62 363 41 011
Fax: 62 363 41 015
e-mail: manggis@alilahotels.com
Website: http://www.alilahotels.com

How to get to Alila Manggis
1½ hours drive from Denpasar Airport to the East coast of Bali. The resort operates its own airport transfer service.

Singapore

Changi International Airport is served by a large number of international and charter airlines. Contact your local Singapore Embassy for visa requirements.

The Sentosa Resort and Spa

2 Bukit Manis Road,
Sentosa,
Singapore 099891,
Singapore
Tel: 65 6275 0331
Fax: 65 6275 0228
e-mail: thesentosa@beaufort.com.sg

Weather
Singapore is hot and humid all year-round destination with little change of temperature. The temperature never drops below 20 and usually climbs to 30 or above during the day. However, as Singapore is a tropical country, at certain times of the year, November–January, there is a heavier rainfall than at others.

How to get to the Sentosa Resort and Spa
A 30 minute drive from Singapore's Changi Airport. Taxis, as well as private cars can enter Sentosa toll-free when a pre-arrangement with the Hotel has been made. The Mass Rapid Transit from Changi Airport to Harbour Front station where the Hotel operates shuttle services, every half hour from the Harbour Front Centre.

Raffles the Plaza

80 Bras Basah Road
Singapore 189560
Tel: 65 6339 7777
Fax: 65 6337 1554
Email: ask-us.plaza-singapore@raffles.com
Website: http://www.singapore-plaza.raffles.com

How to get to Raffles the Plaza
Raffles the Plaza is just 20 minutes away from Singapore Changi International Airport and located above of one the major stations (City Hall station) of the Mass Rapid Transit (Subway) system.

From Changi Airport, take the East Coast Expressway (ECP) and exit at the Rochor Road exit. Turn left onto Beach Road. Raffles The Plaza is on the junction of Beach Road and Bras Basah Road. The hotel operates its own airport transfer service.